MARX,
HAYEK,
AND
UTOPIA

F. A. Hayek
(1899-1992)

Karl Marx
(1818-1883)

MARX,
HAYEK,
AND
UTOPIA

Chris Matthew Sciabarra

State University of New York Press

SUNY Series in the Philosophy of the Social Sciences
Lenore Langsdorf, Editor

Photo of Karl Marx, courtesy of International Publishers.
Photo of F. A. Hayek, courtesy of Institute for Humane Studies.

Published by
State University of New York Press, Albany

For information, address State University of New York
Press, State University Plaza, Albany, N.Y., 12246

Production by E. Moore
Marketing by Bernadette LaManna

Library of Congress Cataloging-in-Publication Data

Sciabarra, Chris Matthew, 1960-
     Marx, Hayek, and utopia / Chris Matthew Sciabarra.
        p.   cm. — (SUNY series in the philosophy of the social
     sciences)
     Includes bibliographical references and index.
     ISBN 0-7914-2615-7 (alk. paper). — ISBN 0-7914-2616-5 (pbk. :
     alk. paper)
        1. Utopias. 2. Dialectic. 3. Radicalism. 4. Social sciences-
     -Philosophy. 5. Marx, Karl, 1818-1883. 6. Hayek, Friedrich A. von
     (Friedrich August), 1899-1992. I. Title. II. Series.
     HX806.S34 1995
     335'.02'0922—dc20
                                                                    94-39676
                                                                        CIP

10 9 8 7 6 5 4 3 2 1

To the memory of my Mom,
for her courage, inspiration, and love.

Contents

Preface

This book derives largely from a portion of my doctoral dissertation, which was completed in 1988. It was initially slated to be published in 1990, by a small *West* German press. Due to economic constraints, the press was unable to publish the book. However, it is not without some irony that the book was initially written when there was a *West* Germany to talk about. Today, some publishers speak quite openly about the difficulty of publishing any books that deal even cursorily with the ideas of Karl Marx. Indeed, in an age that has seen the withering away of the Communist bloc, there seems to be a similarly constituted reaction against the idea of a radical social science. It is as if the fall of Communism offers proof of the failure of the radical project, with which, rightly or wrongly, Marx has been identified. In light of these intellectual developments, I am pleased that my book is finally making its appearance as part of the State University of New York Press Series in the Philosophy of the Social Sciences.

Though I am ultimately responsible for the final product, no book is complete without an acknowledgment of those who have helped in its construction—financially, intellectually, and spiritually. This book benefited from the commentary of a diverse group of scholars. For their helpful guidance, I would like to thank some of the members of my dissertation committee: Gisbert Flanz, Ronald Replogle, Mario Rizzo, and especially, Bertell Ollman. Indeed, no scholar has more influenced my own understanding and appreciation of dialectics than Bertell Ollman. I would also like to thank Don Lavoie, of George Mason University, and Jeffrey Friedman, editor of *Critical Review*, both of whom offered many invaluable comments on important aspects of the manuscript. My gratitude also to Peter Boettke, Douglas Rasmussen, Barry Smith, Karen Vaughn, and several anonymous reviewers for their constructive commentary.

Thanks also to: Laura Glenn, copyeditor; Lenore Langsdorf, Editor of the SUNY Series in the Philosophy of the Social Sciences;

Elizabeth Moore, SUNY Production Editor; Clay Morgan, SUNY Editor; and Judy Spevack and Bernadette LaManna of the SUNY Marketing Department.

I would also like to thank: the Politics Department of New York University, with special acknowledgment to Steve Faulkner, Farhad Kazemi, Kenneth King, Marilyn LaPorte, and Richard Randall; the Herbert H. Lehman Foundation; the Charlotte W. Newcombe Foundation; Inter-University Associates; and the Institute for Humane Studies, with special ackowledgment to Chris Blundell, Walter Grinder, Leonard Liggio, and Jeremy Shearmur.

Finally, I wish to express my deepest gratitude to my family and friends—too numerous to mention individually—for their boundless love and support.

Introduction

Ah, but a man's reach should exceed his grasp,
Or what's a heaven for?
                                        —Robert Browning

There is much truth in Browning's poetic tribute to human possibility. In their attempts to shape their own destiny, people must often aim higher than the ordinary, exhibiting a passionate commitment to the actualization of all that inspires them. And yet, the history of humanity is replete with tragedy, as people have failed to realize their utopian dreams. For in their eagerness to construct a better world, human beings often forget that they are greatly conditioned by the broad context within which they live and function. This context forms the basis for what is possible, just as it defines what is impossible.

In this book I explore the distinction between the possible and the impossible—between the radical and the utopian—through a comparative analysis of the works of Karl Marx and F. A. Hayek. What is immediately significant about this provocative comparison is that the followers of Marx and Hayek have been generally dismissive of one another's views. Each side has expressed the conviction that the other is dismally wrong. However, it is my belief that each has a great deal to learn from the other: Hayekians, who dismiss Marx as a utopian, might detect a significant anti-utopian dimension in his thought; Marxists, who dismiss Hayek as an apologist for capitalism, might discover a certain dialectical sensibility in his thought.

Both Marx and Hayek indict utopianism for its fundamentally nonradical method of theorizing. For both thinkers, the radical is that which seeks to get to the root of social problems, building the realm of the possible out of the conditions that exist. By contrast, the utopian is, by definition, the impossible (the word, strictly translated, means "no-place"). For both Marx and Hayek, utopians internalize an abstract, exaggerated sense of human possibility, aiming to create new social formations based upon a pretense of knowledge. In their blueprints for the ideal society, utopians presuppose that people can master all the sophisticated complexities of social life. Even when their social and ethical ends are decidedly progressive, utopians often rely on reactionary means. They manifest an inherent bias toward the statist construction of alternative institutions in their attempts to practically implement their rationalist abstractions. Both the Marxian and Hayekian perspectives agree that utopianism:

1. fails to take into account the social and historical context of the society that exists;
2. fails to recognize the internal relationship between the theorist and his or her sociohistorical setting;
3. reifies human rationality as a capacity abstracted from social and historical specificity;
4. depends on constructivist rationalism to bridge the gap between conscious human purposes and unintended social consequences; and
5. fails to appreciate the complexity of social action that is constituted by both articulated and tacit elements.

And yet, despite their common anti-utopianism, Marx and Hayek differ with regard to some crucially important epistemic premises. For Hayek, Marx's vision of the ideal communist society rests on the mistaken assumption that in the future, people will be capable of mastering their own destiny. In Hayek's view, this grandiose Marxist illusion served as an ideological legitimation for modern attempts to achieve the millennium through the coercive power of the state. Hayek explains that for important ontological and epistemological reasons, such a utopian goal must engender dystopian consequences. For Marxists, however, any such epistemic constraints are historically specific to capitalism. Such critics as Hilary Wainwright contend that Hayek embraces a "dogmatically individualist" view of knowledge that does not recognize the potential for efficacious collective action.

Despite their differences, both Marx and Hayek embrace a profoundly anti-utopian mode of inquiry. Marx identified this method as dialectics. His own use of dialectical conceptual tools represented the apotheosis of genuinely radical social theorizing. Indeed, Marx's insightful critique of his utopian contemporaries was a reflection of this dialectical approach.

To suggest that Marx's method was radical and anti-utopian is not as controversial as the suggestion of certain "dialectical" elements in Hayek's approach to the social sciences. But if Hayekians have not well appreciated Marx's anti-utopianism, Marxists have yet to acknowledge Hayek's dialectical savvy. This assertion will strike most readers as odd. Hayek, so closely linked to political "conservatism," has never been associated with the dialectical tradition. Dialectics, as Marx reminds us, is "in its essence critical and revolutionary."[1]

It has long been supposed that Marxism is the only legitimate "critical and revolutionary" perspective. This viewpoint was fully articulated in 1919, by the philosopher and literary critic, Georg Lukács. Lukács argued that Marxism *is* dialectics, and that even if all research disproved Marx's individual theses, it would not alter the veracity of his scientific method.[2] Such an identity between Marxism and dialectics implied that non-Marxists were inherently nonradical because they embraced nondialectical methods of inquiry.

But this book suggests that the dialectical approach is not a peculiarly Marxist legacy; it is the birthright of anyone who seeks a more integrated view of social reality than that offered by arid, one-dimensional, ahistorical, utopian models of human behavior. By noting elements of a common dialectical, anti-utopian sensibility in Marxian *and* Hayekian thought, this book begins a worthwhile dialogue between disparate theoretical traditions, aiming for an articulation of their respective contributions and limitations. Through such interaction, each tradition can critically reflect on the strengths and weaknesses of its opponent—and of itself.

Now, the question is: What precisely is meant by "dialectics"?[3]

Throughout the history of philosophy, the term "dialectics" has been used in many different senses. Aristotle recognized dialectic and rhetoric as counterparts of one another; for him, rhetoric was the art of public speaking, or the "faculty of observing in any given case the available means of persuasion," whereas dialectic was the art of logical discussion and argumentation.[4] In dialectic, the interlocutor proceeds from accepted propositions and argues toward a conclusion that is more basic. While mastery of this dialectic technique was the hallmark of Socratic and Platonic philosophy, Aristotle argued that it was insufficient for establishing scientific truth.[5] Nevertheless, he valued dialectic because it demanded the study of questions from multiple vantage points. It is for this reason, perhaps, that Marx, Engels, and Lenin recognized Aristotle as the father of dialectical inquiry. Engels in fact, called Aristotle "the Hegel of the ancient world" who "had already analyzed the most essential forms of dialectic thought."[6] And Lenin argued that within Aristotle lies "the living germs of dialectics *and inquiries* about it."[7]

More than two thousand years after Aristotle's death, Hegel developed a conception of dialectics as an ontological and historical process. Hegel's dialectical method affirms the impossibility of logical contradiction, while focusing instead on *relational* "contradictions" or paradoxes revealed in the dynamism of history. For Hegel opposing concepts are merely partial views whose apparent contradictions could be transcended by exhibiting them as internally related within a larger whole. From pairs of opposing theses, elements of truth could be extracted and integrated into a third position. Other philosophers saw this form of dialectics as a triadic movement in which the conflict of "thesis" and "antithesis" is resolved through "synthesis."[8] "Dialectical materialists" placed this process on an economic foundation, and used it as the basis for a philosophy of history.

The best way in which to understand the dialectical impulse is to view it as a *method* of social inquiry. In any approach to the social sciences, there is always a certain reciprocity between the method and the content—the "how" and the "what"—of one's analysis. In this book, I am less concerned with any sustained polemic defending or attacking the specific *content* of Marxian and/or Hayekian social theory. I focus primarily on the dialectical methods that underlie their divergent theories. *How* Marx and Hayek conceptualize social reality very much affects *what* factors they see at work. Likewise, *what* Marx and Hayek observe in social reality simultaneously affects *how* they think about it. In many instances, these thinkers exhibit *both* methodological and substantive similarities. But it is primarily from the vantage point of method, that both thinkers have uncovered an intellectual hubris at the base of utopian politics.

As employed by both Marx and Hayek, the dialectical method preserves the analytical integrity and organic unity of the whole. While it recommends study of the whole from the vantage point of any part, it eschews reification, that is, it avoids the abstraction of a part from the whole and its illegitimate conceptualization as a whole unto itself. The dialectical method recognizes that what is separable in thought is not separable in reality.

Moreover, dialectics requires the examination of the whole both systemically (or "synchronically") and historically (or "diachronically"). From a synchronic perspective, it grasps the parts as systemically interrelated, both constituting the whole, while being constituted by it. Diachronically, dialectics grasps that any system emerges over time, that it has a past, a present, and a future. It refuses to disconnect factors, events, problems, and issues from each other or from the system which they jointly constitute. It views social problems not discretely, but in terms of the root conditions which they both reflect and sustain. A dialectical mode of analysis recognizes the internal relationship between goals and context, and seeks a resolution that is immanent to the conditions that exist. Ultimately, then, the dialectical thinker seeks not merely to critically understand the system, but to alter it fundamentally.

While it is well recognized that Marx employed dialectical methods in his work, it is also true that Hayek embraced certain critical aspects of a dialectical method. Hayek opposed the deliberate construction of institutional designs in disregard of historical context. He saw social evolution as a by-product of both articulated and unarticulated practices. He viewed social institutions as historically constituted by both human intentionality and the unintended consequences of social action. He provided a fundamentally nonrationalistic groundwork from which there might be gleaned an alternative, non-Marxist radicalism.

In Part One of this book, I begin my reconstruction of the Hayekian critique of utopianism. Chapter One places Hayek's thought in its proper historical and methodological context. Hayek's evolutionist perspective synthesizes elements from the classical liberal and classical conservative traditions. It transcends the dualism between dogmatic, externalist, atomistic individualism and strict, collectivistic organicity.

Chapter Two focuses on a major substantive issue in historical investigation: the deep polarity in the historical process between the conscious intentions of human actors and the unintended consequences of human action. In this chapter, I introduce Hayek's formal critique of "constructivist rationalism," which constitutes the epistemological foundation for the modern social-engineering state.

Chapter Three examines Hayek's critique of constructivism in much greater detail, placing special emphasis on the distinction between the articulated and tacit dimensions of knowledge. Specific attention is paid to Hayek's integration of the important contributions of Michael Polanyi and Karl Popper.

In Part Two, Hayek's critique is engaged with its Marxian adversary. Quite apart from the substantive validity of their theories, it is the organic, historical, and contextual quality of their dialectical methods that provides them with a broad analytical range, a highly integrated awareness of systemic interconnections, and a provocative basis for comparison.

Long predating Hayek, it was Karl Marx who first disparaged utopianism for its futility. In many ways, Marx's opposition to utopian socialism bears a remarkable similarity to the Hayekian critique of constructivism. My discussion in Part Two traces the Marxian argument through a succession of theoretical stages. The dialectic, besides being the methodological framework for Marx's critique of utopianism, is also the means by which Marx envisions a triumph over dualism, specifically, a transcendence of the polarity between human action and unintended social consequences. Marx is acutely aware of the Hayekian concern for socio-historical context. He recognizes institutional order as the product of human action but not of deliberate human design. Much, if not all, of Marx's major theoretical concepts, can be interpreted as the means by which he grasps the systemic and historical peculiarities of the capitalist mode of production, a social formation that is not amenable to the control of conscious human agency.

Because so much has been written about Marx, and because it is impossible to survey all of the myriad interpretations that have emerged throughout the textual history of Marxism, it is necessary to acknowledge one's basic assumptions. This book categorically rejects the view of such thinkers as Althusser and Hook that there is a theoretical or "epistemological break" between the young and the mature Marx. While Marx changed his theoretical emphasis at different points in his intellectual evolution, there is a basic unity that encompasses his project. Marx may have presented a more philosophical expression of his developing views in his younger years, but it is a major error to conclude that his mature "materialistic" perspective departs from his earlier formulations. Marx begins in the abstract realm of Young Hegelianism, and moves toward a more concrete exposition of the same approach in his historical materialism.[9]

The epistemologically fragmented reading of Marx's works has promoted deep divisions in the left academy between "subjectivist" and "objectivist" orientations. The dichotomy was made inevitable by the different polemical writings of both Marx and Engels. This polemicism has led some theorists to focus on single strands in

Marx's works and to reify the part into the whole.[10] Thus, the subjectivist orientation is characteristically phenomenological, humanistic, and decidedly, Hegelian, while the objectivists are more positivistic, scientistic, and deterministic.[11]

Newer writers in the Marxist tradition, among them, Bertell Ollman, Carol Gould, Scott Meikle, and Kevin Brien,[12] have emphasized the multidimensionality of Marx's thought, identifying the subjectivist and objectivist interpretations as fundamentally flawed. One-dimensional readings of Marx neglect the integrated character of his project, which encompasses *both* materialistic and idealistic factors, "base" and "superstructure," existential parameters and free human choice. None of these is isolable from the other. Each is in an organic unity with its counterpart.

A one-dimensional interpretation of Marx's project emerges from a misapprehension of the nature of his method of inquiry. In presenting his economic theories in the first volume of *Capital*, Marx maintained:

> the method of presentation must differ in form from that of inquiry. The latter has to appropriate the material in detail, to analyse its different forms of development, to trace out their inner connexion. Only after this work is done, can the actual movement be described.[13]

How Marx describes and presents his theories depends on the audience he is addressing. Each audience has its own distinctive way of thinking, its own interests and knowledge, and Marx takes each of these factors into account.[14] Knowledge of his audience largely determines the character of Marx's presentation.[15]

Based on this observation, Ollman has argued persuasively that Marx's works are successive approximations to his full intellectual reconstruction. Marx views the phenomena in capitalist society from different vantage points and on different levels of generality. He often presents his findings to vastly different audiences. Hence, in some more polemical moments, Marx's theory resembles a strict technological or economic determinism. The error, Ollman explains, lies in accepting any particular one-sided exposition as the "full cloth" of Marx's intellectual reconstruction.[16]

Given the intimate personal and intellectual relationship between Marx and Engels, I must also reject the argument that Engels is primarily responsible for these one-sided distortions of Marx's thought.[17] Marx and Engels should not be treated as one and the same; neither should they be viewed as intrinsically opposed. While Engels's works are employed regularly in this book, they are used selectively as a means of supporting or clarifying the points made originally by Marx. In some cases, Engels offers explanations that are clearer and more precise than those provided by Marx himself. His letters in the 1890s, for instance, are superb clarifications of dialectical method.

My exposition of Marx's perspective begins in Chapter Four with an examination of his critique of dualism. Marx's thought is itself a conscious product of this critique. Hence, it is imperative to first present the critique of dualism, which is both the object and basis of Marx's dialectical mode of analysis.

In Chapter Five, I examine the Marxian dialectic and its reliance on a doctrine of internal relations. Internalism does not view a thing as isolated or static, since its conditions of existence and its relationship with other things are definitional of its nature. One might presume that future communist society would be just as internally integrated and multidimensional as the very concepts that Marx utilizes.

In exploring that vision of communism, Chapter Six concentrates on the provocative clash between Marxian and Hayekian perspectives. The book concludes with Chapter Seven, and a brief investigation of the Marxian resolution as reconstructed by contemporary theorists, such as Jürgen Habermas and Hilary Wainwright. Habermas makes explicit the epistemological basis of Marx's ideal society in which collective humanity produces the desired effects. This projection of broad-based social efficacy is all-encompassing. For Habermas it stretches even into the realm of symbolic interaction and implies the full articulation of the tacit dimension of knowledge. Wainwright, on the other hand, has attempted to answer directly the challenge of Hayek and "the free-market right." Her "arguments for a new left" derive from Marxian and Habermasian premises, while being far more cognizant of Hayekian strictures. Ultimately, any attempt to reconstruct the radical project must recognize and resolve the very real tension between epistemic limits and socially transformative potentials.

In the excursion that follows, it is my hope that the Marxian and Hayekian intellectual traditions can be engaged fruitfully. Reaching beyond the provincialism of each, grasping their commonalities, this book aims to explicate the profound differences between a radical and a utopian approach to social theory.

PART ONE

Hayek and the
Critique of Utopianism

1 Hayekian Dialectics

As an economist of the Austrian school, Hayek received the Nobel Prize in 1974. Yet, his perspective goes beyond the constraints of economic science. Through his integration of evolutionist theory with elements of a dialectical method, Hayek presents one of the most powerful critiques of utopianism in the history of social and political thought.

Transcending Conservatism and Liberalism

Hayek was part of a contemporary evolutionist tradition that includes theorists such as Michael Polanyi and Karl Popper. This tradition has often been characterized as conservative. John Plamenatz argues that such conservatism is neither a revolt against social change nor a desire to preserve the status quo. On a broader, philosophical level, in Plamenatz's view, a conservative

> believes that the ability to make large social changes according to plan is severely limited, and that the attempt to make them ordinarily does more harm than good.[1]

It is perhaps, on this basis, that Popper has expressed great affection for conservatism. His critique of utopianism is directed against all forms of "radical" politics. He denigrates such "radical" change as utopian, ahistorical, drastic, and destructive.[2] Popper would agree with Russell Kirk who writes that conservatism recognizes change as a "process independent of conscious human endeavor." Kirk contends that "Human reason and speculation" are capacities that can only be utilized "in a spirit of reverence, awake to their own fallibility."[3] Based on this description, all contemporary evolutionism can be seen as a product of the "conservative mind."

Yet there is an important distinction between Hayek and others in the evolutionist tradition. Unlike Popper, Hayek did not equate radicalism with utopianism. He recognized the important link between the radical project and evolutionist insights. He argued that utopian thought gave no such recognition. It was inherently ahistorical and noncontextual.

Hayek's dissent from Popperian antiradicalism suggests an approach that is neither conservative nor liberal. Hayek combined key elements from both Burkean conservatism and Scottish liberalism. Politically, however, Hayek opposed contemporary American conservative ideology. He condemned conservatism as "paternalistic, nationalistic, and power-adoring . . . traditionalistic, anti-intellectual and often mystical."[4] In *The Constitution of Liberty*, for example, Hayek saw a connection between conservatives and socialists who would use coercion and arbitrary power in support of their respective values. Conservatism, for Hayek, was too fearful of change and much too fond of authority.[5]

Hayek's neoliberal or quasi-libertarian political and economic philosophy opposes government intervention on behalf of business or labor. Hayek saw the growth of monopoly as a corporativist by-product,

> a deliberate collaboration of organized capital and organized labor where the privileged groups of labor share in the monopoly profits at the expense of the community and particularly at the expense of the poorest, those employed in the less-well-organized industries and the unemployed.[6]

Hayek believed that he had much more in common with progressive socialists on specific social issues than with conservatives. He agreed with socialists on most questions of value. Yet, he opposed central planning because it was both counterproductive and subversive of its own stated ultimate ends.[7] In a unique synthesis, Hayek integrated a classical liberal commitment to the free market, a classical conservative commitment to evolutionism, and elements of a profoundly radical, dialectical method of social inquiry.

The classical liberal revolutions of the seventeenth and eighteenth centuries were complex historical phenomena with broad consequences. The power of the liberal worldview derived from its passionate attack on the legitimacy of the dissolving Old Order, its mysticism, quasi-feudalism and mercantilist privilege. In bolstering the development of competitive capitalism, liberalism embraced an ideology of natural rights, individualism, limited government, and private property. It also provoked the ire of conservatives who sought to protect the traditions of the past and the stability of the status quo from the onslaught of liberal doctrine.

For Edmund Burke the excesses of the French Revolution constituted a dangerous threat to civilized humanity. Burke argued that unlike the French, the English used their past as the stepping stone to a "glorious" future, preserving monarchy and liberty alike. Burke believed that violent revolution destroyed existing institutions, substituting despotism and anarchy for communal unity and evolutionary reform. The revolutionaries, in their demands for the rights of man, proposed a rationalist design for a new society that neglected people's religious passions, habits, and traditions. Rights are of little consequence, claimed Burke, when severed from the context of political and social continuity, essential prerequisites for the establishment of any social order. As Robert Nisbet explains:

> Modern political conservatism takes its origins in Burke's insistence upon the rights of society and its historically formed groups such as family, neighborhood, guild and church against the "arbitrary power" of a political government. For Burke, individual liberty is only possible within the context of a plurality of social authorities, of moral codes and of historical traditions, all of which, in organic articulation, serve at one and the same time as "the inns and resting places" of the human spirit and the intermediary barriers to the power of the state over the individual.[8]

Burke was not against change. He offered instead, a principled opposition to the rationalist quest for "earthly utopias of human design."[9] Burke's support for more favorable treatment of the American and Indian colonies demonstrated the reformist character of his politics.[10] He maintained that social emergencies allowed for deviations from traditional principles within certain limits. While deviations from a fixed rule were necessary under these circumstances, they were not to be affected through the "decomposition of the whole civil and political mass for the purpose of originating a new civil order out of the first elements of society." In a classic celebration of English tradition, Burke wrote: "A state without the means of some change is without the means of its conservation." It is the English who "look upon the legal hereditary succession of their crown as among their rights, not as among their wrongs; as a benefit, not as a grievance, as security for their liberty, not as a badge of servitude." Such an evolutionary process is of "inestimable value" in preserving the "stability and perpetuity" of the system.[11]

Burke was not alone in his reverence for the stabilizing influence of tradition. His English and Scottish liberal predecessors and contemporaries were in fact, not advocates of "atomistic" individualism. Locke for instance, never embraced such atomism, since he saw social institutions such as the family, the voluntary association, and the church as mediating human existence and providing a setting for sociability and community.[12] Louis Hartz maintains in *The Liberal Tradition in America*, that in the United States, for example, there was an integration of Burke and Locke. This monolithic legacy combined "rock-ribbed traditionalism with high inventiveness," and "ancestor worship with ardent optimism."[13] Yet, Hartz's thesis obscures the basic continuity between classical conservative and classical liberal thought. Both were expressive of the spontaneous character of the emerging capitalist social order.

Burkean conservatism and Scottish liberalism were of the same cloth; both were distinctly appropriate and relevant to their particular social and historical context. The rising English merchant class developed a great pride in the evolutionary quality of the common law and in the social and economic institutions that protected the liberties and rights of Englishmen. Burkean conservatives and Scottish liberals stressed evolution, while the French rationalists demanded revolution. Burkean conservatives and Scottish liberals upheld the superior wisdom of tradition, custom, and habit, while incipient capitalism was bringing about a gradual dissolution of traditional social bonds. In their calls for gradual, evolved reform, the English and Scottish thinkers emphasized the importance of historical evolution to the development of social institutions. They opposed the notion that people could step outside the historical process and redesign the civil order "out of the first elements of society" through the infinite powers of their Reason.

Each of the Scottish liberals offered a variation on the theme of evolutionary order. Adam Ferguson argued that the commercial society emerges through human interaction but not through "the execution of any human design." Bernard Mandeville suggested too, that social institutions were the unintended product of human interaction. Sir Matthew Hale claimed that the emergent order constituted a complex whole that could not be comprehended by a single mind. Both Adam Smith and David Hume wrote of the system of natural liberty in which people were led, in the words of Smith, "as if by an invisible hand" to serve the public interest when this was clearly no part of their intention. Hume outlined the nonrational customs and habits that were the basis of artificial rules and laws preserving the "stability of possessions." This common law tradition showed far greater wisdom than any rationalist legal theory. Its complexity could not possibly be duplicated by the a priori maxims of designed legality.[14]

Hayek versus "Methodological Individualism"

The evolutionist perspective was carried on in the nineteenth century by thinkers such as Gustave de Molinari, Herbert Spencer, Frederic Bastiat, and Carl Menger. It finds its most developed form in the twentieth century in the writings of Hayek, Polanyi, and Popper. Indeed, these three thinkers have often relied on one another's contributions, constituting a distinctive contemporary evolutionist school. Hayek's own thought in particular, exhibits a Burkean distrust of French rationalism in its "contempt for tradition, custom, and history in general." Rationalists believe that "man's reason alone should enable him to construct society anew."[15] Hayek opposes this exaggerated conception of human cognitive efficacy. His framework reflects a deep appreciation for organic social interrelationships and their dynamic development over time. Hayek writes:

> The picture of man as a being who, thanks to his reason, can rise above the values of his civilization, in order to judge it from the outside or from a higher point of view, is an illusion. It simply must be understood that reason itself is part of civilization. All we can ever do is to confront one part with the other parts. Even this process leads to incessant movement, which may in the very long course of time change the whole. But sudden complete reconstruction of the whole is not possible at any stage of the process, because we must always use the material that is available, and which itself is the integrated product of a process of evolution.[16]

A transcendental view of the whole is not possible because the individual is among the elements that both constitute and are constituted by the social whole itself. An individual human being can always examine a particularized aspect of culture that gives him or her a certain perspective on the whole. But the individual's particularized vantage point emerges within the context of the culture, not external to it. Since we are unable to get a synoptic view as impersonal, detached social actors, we have it in our power to "tinker with parts of a given whole" but never to "entirely redesign it."[17]

Popper, like Hayek, also opposes the utopian notion of ahistorical social change:

> One cannot begin a new social system by wiping a canvas clean. The painter and those who cooperate with him as well as the institutions which make their life possible, his dreams and plans for a better world, his standards of decency and morality, are all part of the social system, i.e., of the picture to be wiped out. If they were really to clean the canvas, they would have to destroy themselves and their utopian plans. The political artist clamours, like Archimedes, for a place outside the social world on which he can take his stand, in order to level it off its hinges. But such a place does not exist; and the social world must continue to function during any reconstruction.[18]

The modern evolutionists focus on internal relations within an organic, social totality. Their methodological approach shares much with the Marxian view.[19] This is a paradoxical proposition since Hayek and Popper have been characterized ordinarily as strict "methodological individualists."[20] Hayek's "methodological individualism" is expressed most clearly in his *Counter-Revolution of Science*, a collection of essays previously published in the early 1940s, and in his *Individualism and Economic Order*, published in 1948.[21] But to focus on these works to the virtual exclusion of Hayek's later writings provides a one-sided view of the Nobel Laureate's integrated method of analysis. It is no coincidence, therefore, that even Wainwright, in her critique of "the free market right," continues to qualify Hayek's approach as "dogmatically individualist."[22] Wainwright's criticisms, while significant, derive primarily from her analysis of Hayek's earlier collections.[23] Over the years, however, Hayek's views developed considerably. His comprehensive evolutionist perspective goes well beyond individualist strictures.

It is important to note however, that "methodological individualism" as such, has often been identified with atomism, reductionism, and ahistoricism. It is said to see the whole as the mere sum of its parts. It views the individual—or the part—as of primary epistemological importance, and structures the whole through an additive analytical process. Some sympathetic interpreters of Hayek have challenged this very notion of methodological individualism while continuing to place Hayek within this very tradition. For instance, Chiaki Nishiyama explains that Hayek's method does not ignore the whole. Rather, it views the whole from the vantage point of the "*interactions* among its constituent factors." These relations between factors are dynamically emergent.[24]

In defending Hayek's approach as individualistic, Nishiyama struggles against typically atomistic caricatures of this methodology. He denies that individualism reduces all social phenomena to mere "collections of their constituent parts."[25] He suggests that individualism is as much interested in grasping the whole as its holistic counterparts. But by retaining this characterization of Hayek's approach, Nishiyama reproduces the traditional polarity between individualistic and holistic alternatives. He inadvertently obscures the profoundly dialectical methodological elements that inform the Hayekian perspective.[26]

It is a distortion to view Hayek's approach as *either* individualistic *or* holistic. Hayek's method is *fundamentally dialectical*, encompassing elements of individualism *and* holism, while repudiating all forms of reductionism, atomism, ahistoricism, and strict organicity. This claim is at once disorienting and provocative. Indeed, Hayek's disciples on the free market right and his critics on the socialist left might view the very notion of "Hayekian dialectics" as an oxymoron. Some commentators have stated that to accuse "Hayek of 'dialectical' affectations . . . would make him turn around in his grave."[27] And yet, a more detailed examination of Hayek's mode of inquiry suggests that the distinguished neoliberal social philosopher was highly dialectical in many significant ways.

Throughout Hayek's writings, there is a crucial emphasis on the importance of historical and systemic context, on the complex, evolving, organic unity of the social world. This understanding is not accidental to Hayek's approach; it forms the core of a sophisticated, nonreductionistic method of social inquiry. Both Hayek and Popper argue against reductionism in the social sciences since society is *more* than the mere sum of its parts. Reductionism relies on a "historical myth," in Popper's view, because it sees human beings as somehow "presocial." As Popper argues, "man's" ancestors were "social prior to being human (since language presupposes society). Men are if anything the product of life in society rather than its creators."[28] And while Hayek recognizes the ontological priority of concrete particulars, of real, existing individuals, he views the whole as a relationally evolving totality that is beyond the capacity of any single individual to fully comprehend. Hayek sees the "individual," "reason," "morality," and "culture" as emergent qualities of social evolution. He maintains that there is no concept of the "individual" that is not tied to a historically and socially specific structure. Sensing an intricate reciprocity between the parts and the whole, Hayek writes:

> The individual with a particular structure and behavior owes its existence . . . to a society of a particular structure because only within such a society has it been advantageous to develop some of its peculiar characteristics, while the order of society in turn is a result of . . . regularities of conduct which the individuals have developed in society.[29]

In this passage, Hayek stresses an organic conjunction or dual causation of individual and social factors. Each factor is both a precondition and a result of the other. Neither factor can exist without the other since each is partly constitutive of the other. Thus, in Hayek's view,

> the structures possessing a kind of order will exist because the elements do what is necessary to secure the persistence of that order . . . the adaptation of the parts to the requirements of the whole becomes a necessary part of the explanation of why structures of the kind exist . . . that the elements behave in a certain way by the circumstance that this sort of conduct is most likely to preserve the whole—on the preservation of which depends the preservation of the individuals, which would therefore not exist if they did not behave in this manner.[30]

Hayek's framework seems to embody a circular logic, but it is illustrative of a dialectical, relational method. Hayek does not reduce a system to its individual components since the structural relationships of a society fit its individual components into a meaningful whole. Social collectivities connect individual activities by intelligible relations.[31] Hayek adamantly opposes atomistic individualism. For Hayek,

> the overall order of actions in a group is in two respects more than the totality of regularities observable in the actions of the

individuals and cannot be wholly reduced to them. *The whole is more than the mere sum of its parts* because it presupposes that the elements are related to each other in a particular manner and because the existence of these relations which are essential for the existence of the whole cannot be accounted for wholly by the interaction of the parts but only by their interaction with an outside world both of the individual parts and the whole.[32] (Emphasis added.)

To see the whole as more than the mere sum of its parts is to see it as fully integrated. The relationships within the social whole are necessarily *internal*, that is, the whole could not be what it is without those relations that give it meaning. Likewise, these relations are significant precisely because of their specific functions within the totality. Hayek agrees with the scientist and philosopher, Michael Polanyi, who argues that "all particulars become meaningless if we lose sight of the pattern which they jointly constitute."[33] For Hayek, there is an *organic* link between the whole and its elements. Indeed, the social totality is best viewed as "an organism in which every part performs a necessary function for the continuance of the whole, without any human mind having devised it."[34] This totality shapes and is shaped by the particular relations that exist.

These dialectical insights illustrate Hayek's debt to Austrian and German philosophy.[35] On an immediate level, Hayek cites the influence of his mentor, Ludwig von Mises, who viewed society as an organism rather than an organization.[36] Hayek also recognizes the similarity of his approach to autopoiesis, cybernetics, homeostasis, synergetics, and systems theory.[37]

John Gray, in his book *Hayek on Liberty*, suggests that Hayek's framework more fundamentally derives from Kant, Mach, Popper, Polanyi, and Wittgenstein. Organic functionalism however, predates each of these thinkers. It can be found even in Aristotle's opposition to reification, his refusal to abstract the particular from its dynamic or systemic context.[38] Such dialectical insights were more fully articulated and developed in the early nineteenth century by Hegel. Yet neither Hayek nor his disciples has formally recognized the methodological parallels with the Hegelian perspective. So too, most contemporary Marxist critics of Hayek remain deeply ignorant of his dialectical mode of analysis.

Popper, however, readily acknowledges "a similarity between Hegel, who considered reason as a social product, and Burke, who talked of our indebtedness and dependence on our social heritage."[39] Given this parallel between two divergent traditions of social thought, it is not surprising that both Marx and Hayek share an insight into the social and historical nature of human institutions and capacities. Both thinkers recognize the principle put forth by Hegel, that the parts are "moments of an organic unity . . . in which each is as necessary as the other." For Hegel, as for Marx and Hayek, such "mutual necessity" is "the life of the whole," and cannot be ignored without causing profound damage to the character—and validity—of one's analysis.[40]

As we shall see, Marx draws his inspiration directly from Hegel, and condemns utopian thought for its abstraction of the part, human reason, from the whole, the context within which human reason gains concrete expression. By focusing on the internally related whole as an organic and historical system, Hayek suggests, like Marx, that each of us is a component part of the totality. This internality prohibits individual members from stepping outside the whole to view it from a synoptic perspective. As such, no individual or group of individuals can undertake a complete restructuring of the society. For both Marx and Hayek, this is what utopianism demands since it removes individuals from their social context, and totalizes the power of reason. Utopian theory rests on the reification of rationality. It abstracts reason from its social and historical specificity, and posits an omniscient grasp of the totality.

Internal Relations

At this juncture, it is valuable to consider the doctrine of internal relations, which is central to all forms of dialectical inquiry. A deeper grasp of internal relations, as explicated by such theorists as Brand Blanshard and Bertell Ollman, can contribute much to our appreciation of Hayek's dialectical sensibility.

There are two basic theories of social relationships: organicism and atomism.[41] The most extreme expression of the former is the doctrine of strict organicity.[42] In a strict organicist approach, the interdependence of social reality makes it impossible to examine any part of existence without taking into account *every* part of existence. Since everything must be known before anything is analyzed, this position affirms that no elements are isolable in principle. All elements are constitutive of a whole within which each of them is internally related to and dependent on the other.[43] Strict organicity sees the whole as greater than the sum of its parts. But it often obscures individual elements as they are completely absorbed and determined by holistic categories of explanation.

Epistemologically, organicist integration offers no criterion by which to identify those core relations that may be essential to the definition of the whole under scrutiny. Strict organicity integrates concepts in disregard of necessity, and fails to focus on the essential characteristics that define the whole. Indeed, it is unable to distinguish between "essential" and "nonessential" characteristics since it regards all elements of the whole as essential to its nature. Strict organicity drops the context of our knowledge, and ultimately depends on omniscience. Since knowledge is an open-ended process, it is, according to this doctrine, never complete. By these standards, our understanding of a whole can never be truly validated as adequate.

As we shall see, dialectics is derived from an organicist view of society. However, it differs from a strict organicist approach in one crucial epistemological sense: dialectics recognizes the organic unity of a whole without seeking to identify all of its elements. Those who use a dialectical method never assume that people can achieve complete knowledge of every constituent and interrelationship within the whole. Indeed, such an omniscient grasp of the whole is impossible. Yet, this is what strict organicity demands: a *metaphysical* identification of the whole and all of its parts. While strict organicity implies a utopian, synoptic comprehension of the totality, the dialectical approach seeks a *contextual* identification of the totality that reflects the limited, historical state of our knowledge.

Atomism is the second basic theory of social relationships. Its most extreme form is the doctrine of strict atomism, in which the world is subdivided and reduced to a mere description of things. All relationships between these separable and isolable things are necessarily external. Hence, the world is constituted by elements that are strictly independent of one another. Strict atomism sees the whole as the additive sum of ever-smaller constituents. Yet, the more remote and microscopic our analysis becomes, the greater is the chance that we will be unable to grasp the interactions of the parts.

For example, seeing an individual person as nothing more than a physiological and chemical mass of cells makes it difficult to define the essential characteristics of human being. Atomism multiplies the number of concepts beyond necessity, losing its grasp of those integrative, complex, and core relations which define the whole. It separates and isolates elements in the whole that may reciprocally presuppose each other.

The organicist-atomist distinction underlies two different modes of sociological "perception," two vastly different ways of perceiving and organizing social reality: dualism versus dialectics.

A theory of perception, writes David Kelley, must take into account the principle that "the object appears in a way that is relative to the means by which we perceive it."[44] This is not a mere tautology. Kelley emphasizes that appearance is the product of a relation between the object that exists and the sensory means by which this object is perceived. Both the object and the subject have an identity which, in their interaction, results in the perception of an existing object in a specific form. The context of our awareness cannot be disconnected from the perception of the object, nor is it distinct from the object. It is not possible to step outside of this context, because we are internal to the process itself.

Kelley defends the theory of perceptual relativity. His realist approach denies the "Cartesian quest for an infallible type of knowledge . . . a form of cognition that is free from conditions, that is not subject to any limitation placed on it."[45] Kelley criticizes this abstract notion of perception as a "diaphanous" model whose basic presupposition is that the object itself determines the way in which people perceive it. This theory of "immaculate perception," as Nietzsche called it, is gravely flawed because it abstracts from the human subject the enormous context within which perception functions.[46] The subject constitutes a perceptual system whose basis is a relational interaction with objects in the world around it. The object itself appears differently depending on the mode of perception.[47]

In an analogous extension of this principle, it might be said that there are different modes of *sociological* perception. The connections and boundaries that we draw between and among the constituent elements of social reality will depend on the modalities which we adopt. *How* we see the world will strongly influence *what* we see. This does not mean, as Kant would have it, that our methodology is subjective, that is, that we impose subjective structures on an objective reality. Rather, it affirms the principle that *vantage point influences perception*.

The fact is, however, that dialectics and dualism are not strictly *perceptual* systems. They are fully developed *conceptual* methods that must be defended in terms of their functional ability to comprehend the objects of their inquiry. Various cultures and philosophical traditions conceptualize differing connections and boundaries between and among the constituent elements of social reality.[48] Dialectics and dualism are two such broad conceptual schemes; their adequacy to reality must be judged ultimately by their capacity to explain the phenomena under investigation.[49]

Dualistic methodology is inspired by an atomistic worldview.[50] Like atomists, dualists emphasize separation, fragmentation, and division. Typically, dualism attempts to distinguish two irreconcilable spheres of social reality, though it often leads theorists to totalize one sphere to the detriment of another. In this regard, one can distinguish between genuine philosophical dualists who see two, co-equal, mutually exclusive spheres in reality, and philosophical monists, who accept the dichotomies defined by dualists, and reduce one polarity to an epiphenomenon of the other.

For the purposes of this study, I have identified two forms of dualism in social theory. Both of these forms see an irreconcilable antagonism between political and civil society, or the state and the market. The first is statist dualism which, in political practice, gives priority to the state apparatus. It promotes an instrumentalist view of the state as a mechanism that can accomplish different tasks relative to its class character. As such, statist dualism—particularly in its socialistic incarnations—views the capitalist state as an instrument of the capitalist class. A workers' state, by contrast, would absorb the sphere of civil society and transcend the alleged exploitation inherent in market relations.

The second form is libertarian dualism. This model is as one-dimensional as its statist counterpart. It grants priority to civil society and views the state as an external intrusion on the market and its coordinative capacities. Whereas statist dualism sees the market as dependent on the state for its survival, libertarian dualism views the state as dependent on the market for its sustenance. Politics is an epiphenomenon of material forces. Libertarian dualism argues that the market can exist without the state, but that the state cannot exist without the market. The state presupposes some form of material production from which it expropriates wealth for its survival. As a contemporary political approach, libertarian dualism is best expressed in anarchocapitalist ideology.[51]

As we shall see, there are certain libertarian dualistic elements suggested in Hayek's framework, particularly in his distinction between "spontaneous" and "designed" order. However, Hayek concentrates far more attention on the integrative relationships within a social whole. He does not view the whole as an abstract or ahistorical totality; rather, he sees the whole as a dynamic historical process and social movement. His method of social inquiry is fundamentally dialectical.

Like dualism, dialectics is a way of thinking. A dialectical perspective, however, focuses not on external connections between static elements, but on dynamic internal relations. These relations constitute and are constituted by the elements of the whole under scrutiny. Ollman writes:

> Dialectics restructures our thinking about reality by replacing the common sense notion of "thing," as something that *has* a history and *has* external connections with other things, with notions of "process," which *contains* its history and possible futures, and "relation," which *contains* as part of what it is its ties with other relations.[52]

Both dialectics and dualism see relational principles at work; it is the quality of the relation which is in question. Dialectical analysis views things as internally related. Dualism views things as externally related. Having used these terms several times in this chapter, it is important to explore the contrast between internalism and externalism. Brand Blanshard explains:

> A given term is internally related to another if in the absence of the relation it could not be what it is. A term is externally related to another if the relation could equally be present or absent while the term was precisely the same.[53]

In social inquiry, an internalist perspective views every aspect as integral to the context such that it cannot be truly conceived or understood apart from this context. Every aspect of the totality is what it is "in virtue of relations to what is other than itself." These relations affect each other in differing degrees. Hence, no investigation will reveal completely the nature of any aspect until the theorist exhausts its relations to all other aspects.[54] Thus, Blanshard defends the doctrine of internal relations. For Blanshard a thing's elements

> are engaged in manifold interactions, by way of attraction and repulsion with things around it, and these almost certainly determine its shape down to the last detail. This particular shape, like this degree of malleability, is not externally related to its other characters; they are bound up with these causally and therefore . . . necessarily.[55]

However, Blanshard concludes that "every character counts, but not all characters count equally."[56] He is crucially aware of the need to assign greater significance to certain factors within the whole so as to avoid the problems of strict organicity. Blanshard argues:

> An organism or a mind is a whole whose parts are more obviously inter-dependent than those of a cloud, but no thing or individual stands by itself; it is what it is in consequence of lines of determination—causal, logical, or both—running out into an illimitable universe.[57]

Blanshard states here, in epistemological terms, what Hayek argues sociologically. The individual, in Hayek's view, cannot stand by himself; he is invariably an actor in a specific historical and cultural context. For Hayek, there is a limit beyond which we are unable to articulate the rules, customs, and habits that govern our lives. We are *internal* to these rules and cannot take an external, transcendental role. Even our consciousness operates according to rules of which we are not conscious, since these rules are *internal* to the operation itself.

Hayek maintains that the mind is inscribed in a cultural setting. It is wrong to apply one-way causal notions to either. The human mind and culture developed concurrently. They are internally related, such that each is a precondition and result of the other. "It is probably no more justified to claim that thinking man created his culture," argues Hayek, "than that culture created his reason."[58] Nonetheless, many thinkers have represented reason as "the capping stone" of human evolution that helped people to design culture. But this notion of reason is highly abstract and rationalistic. It obscures the interpersonal, social process in which reasoning people both absorb and transmit cultural values. Hayek states, in almost Marxian fashion, that social theory must start "from men whose whole nature and character is determined by their existence in society." Social interaction creates effects that are greater than any individual mind "can ever fully comprehend."[59]

This view reached its apex in Hayek's book, *The Fatal Conceit*. Hayek reaffirms his conviction that civilization arises not from human design or intention, but spontaneously, as people conform to certain traditions, rules, and moral practices. For Hayek, these customs stand "between instinct and reason," since, from a logical, psychological, and temporal viewpoint, they are neither the direct result of instinctual patterns nor of reasoned deliberation. The mind is a product of cultural evolution and as such, its reasoning capacity has developed concurrently with all other aspects of culture. "It is not our intellect that created our morals," writes Hayek, "rather, human interactions governed by our morals make possible the growth of reason and those capabilities associated with it."[60]

Hayek maintains that while human beings are purposeful actors, their behavior is rule-governed. Civilization itself, developed out of the human capacity to follow rules.[61] In Hayek's view, "culture is a tradition of learnt rules of conduct which have never been 'invented' and whose functions the acting individuals usually do not understand."[62] Even an individual's cognitive capacity advances on the basis of social tools of learning embodied in a particular culture's language. Each language supplies us with "a framework of our thinking within which we henceforth move without being aware of it."[63]

That Hayek's viewpoint borders on social determinism is certainly a viable objection. In Chapter Two I argue that, on balance, the Hayekian framework is nondeterminist. Hayek views the social order as a constellation of both human intentions and unintended social consequences.

Hayek's framework has been criticized too, for its "relativism."[64] Yet, if viewed as an outgrowth of Hayek's assumptions about the organic interrelationships within social reality, his "relativism" translates into relationism. Hayek states that "the rule one ought to follow in a given society and in particular circumstances in order to produce the best consequences, may not be the best rule in another society where the system of generally adapted rules is different."[65] As Gray observes, Hayek is not invoking the macroscopic evolutionary process as a standard for resolving moral dilemmas. He is, however, recognizing our moral values as the outcome of social evolution, custom, and tradition.[66] These values are cultural artifacts.

Ever the social scientist, Hayek is less interested in moralizing and far more interested in reconstructing cultural and moral traditions so as to understand their functional capacities. These traditions fulfill important social needs. They

> serve an existing factual order which no individual has the power to change fundamentally, because such change would require changes in the rules which other members of the society obey, in part unconsciously or out of sheer habit, and

which, if a viable society of a different type were to be created, would have to be replaced by other rules which nobody has the power to make effective. There can, therefore, be no absolute system of morals independent of the kind of social order in which a person lives, and the obligation incumbent upon us, to follow certain rules derives from the benefits we owe to the order in which we live.[67]

Despite Hayek's view of the finite powers of reason, he argues that revisions in morality can be made only through immanent rational criticism, in which recognizable defects are altered by "analysing the compatibility and consistency of their parts." Through such piecemeal analysis, Hayek admits a certain limited role for the use of reason in the definition of morality. As Hayek explains, human "reason may, although with caution and in humility, and in a piecemeal way, be directed to the examination, criticism and rejection of traditional institutions and moral principles."[68]

What Hayek objects to is the rationalist impulse to recast the whole of our cultural and moral system. In Hayek's view, this would require a gargantuan study of many complex historical and social factors. Though we may be aware of the relevance of our values to the culture in which we live, we are often ignorant of "the particular conditions to which the values we hold are due." Particular values could be explained only if we knew all those relevant historical facts which have coalesced in a unique fashion to produce a particular moral configuration.[69] Hayek doubts the feasibility of such a reconstruction for the same reasons that he dismisses all utopian theorizing.

Though Hayek and Blanshard share a commitment to internal relations, there is a distinctive difference between them. The Hayekian perspective avoids explicitly the pitfalls of strict organicity. As an Absolute Idealist, Blanshard takes cognizance of Hegel's famous description of the development of the bud into a flower. Blanshard explains:

Consider the growth of a flower. Within the bud there is a certain pattern or arrangement of parts; a week later when the bud has burst into bloom, the arrangement is very different; sepals, petals, and stamens are now developed and distinct. Here the first system has evolved into the other, but it is evident that the process is not one of adding part to part while the original nucleus is untouched. It is general and correlated change. Every change among the stamens is balanced by one in the sepals and petals, so that a botanist who was expert enough could tell from the stage of development of any of these precisely what to expect in all the others. At every stage in the process the parts are so related that a change in any one of them is reflected throughout the whole. Here is a type of system whose development clearly proceeds by degrees.[70]

Like Blanshard, Hayek grasps that even a subtle change in a single aspect of a system will redound throughout the whole, and that a gradual change in the whole will be reflected in the network of its constituent parts. But unlike Blanshard, and unlike many internalists, Hayek emphasizes certain strictures on our capacity to know. Blanshard admits that internalists "usually . . . hold that everything, *if we knew enough*, would turn out to be internally related to everything else"[71] (emphasis added). Hayek never assumes that we can know precisely the relational constitution of a social whole. Nor does he assume that we can fully assess the complex changes that emerge as the unintended consequences of our social actions. For Hayek a recognition of systemic interdependence does not culminate in Absolute Idealism. Such a recognition does not imply that one can grasp exhaustively the specific nature of constituted relations. Ultimately, Hayek's understanding of the sophisticated network of internal, social relations leads him to eschew any institutional interference with the network. The attempt to fully know and master the social whole is at the core of modern constructivist rationalism.

It is in his critique of rationalism that Hayek has uncovered a profound paradox at the foundation of utopian theory: a simultaneous dependence on *both* the internality of strict organicity *and* the externality of a dualistic worldview. Utopians seem to recognize that the social totality is composed of infinite internal relationships. Since their vision of change is totalistic, utopians would have to possess perfect knowledge of *every* internal relationship and organic link within the totality in order to reconstruct the society. Hayek emphasizes that such strict organicity is dependent on an illusory omniscience.

And yet, if utopians presume they can acquire knowledge of a strictly organic totality, their own synoptic viewpoint is necessarily exempted from this totality. In seeking to grasp and transform the many *internal* relations within an organic whole, utopians act as if they are *externally* related to that whole. They refuse to recognize

their own contextuality, and ultimately embrace crude constructivism as a social panacea. In twentieth-century politics, such constructivism is exemplified in the social-engineering state, in which
the dualistic polarity of state and civil society is resolved one-dimen-
sionally, by statist brutality.

2 Utopian Intentions and Unintended Consequences

The essence of Hayek's view of social evolution is captured in the introduction to his work, *The Fatal Conceit*. Hayek writes:

> Our civilisation depends, not only for its origin but also for its preservation, on . . . the extended order of human cooperation, an order more commonly, if somewhat misleadingly, known as capitalism . . . [an] extended order [which] resulted not from human design or intention but spontaneously: it arose from unintentionally conforming to certain traditional and largely *moral* practices, many of which men tend to dislike, whose significance they usually fail to understand, whose validity they cannot prove, and which have nonetheless fairly rapidly spread by means of an evolutionary selection—the comparative increase of population and wealth—of those groups that happened to follow them.[1]

Though stated with simplicity, this perspective involves many complex issues. It is not my intention to justify the substantive validity of Hayekian evolutionism, nor do I believe that Hayek has provided a full justification for each of his arguments. Indeed, there are many areas where Hayek's social theory is highly problematic and theoretically weak. Here, I focus specific attention on the epistemological dimensions of Hayek's social theory that have profound implications for his critique of utopianism.

The Unintended Consequences of Social Action

In the above passage, Hayek identifies a deep polarity in the historical process between the conscious intentions of human actors and the unintended consequences of social interaction, a profound tension between the goals of designed institutions and the resulting spontaneity of an evolving order. Hayek characterizes this as a distinction between "designed" and "spontaneous" order. He defines "order" as

> a state of affairs in which a multiplicity of elements of various kinds are so related to each other that we may learn from our acquaintance with some spatial or temporal part of the whole to form correct expectations concerning the rest.[2]

Order is an emergent, organic unity, in which no element exists apart from the whole. Each element affects and is affected by the others, jointly constituting and being constituted by the whole. However, since Hayek rejects strict organicity as a methodological premise, he argues that we can never gain a synoptic understanding of the whole. We can only grasp the structure of social order from a specific vantage point within the totality.

Thus, Hayek extends his dialectical presuppositions into the sociological realm. He views social order as an emergent, complex relationship between human intentionality and unintended social consequences. Even our deliberate efforts to bring about an arranged social order must take place within the broader context of social formations that are not the direct result of deliberate invention.[3] Human interaction over time engenders a framework of general rules that evolves organically and spontaneously. For Hayek, civilization is both a product and process of evolution, a dynamic context for social action.[4] Popper expresses this same sentiment when he states:

> the structure of our social environment is man-made—not consciously designed or explicable in terms of needs, hopes or motives . . . even those which arise as the result of conscious and intentional human actions are, as a rule, the indirect, the unintended, and often the unwanted by-products of such actions.[5]

The dichotomy between the intended and unintended consequences of human action is recognized and universally accepted among social scientists in a variety of disciplines. Nevertheless, there are some important philosophical issues that are relevant to this distinction. Since it is questionable if we ever truly know the intentions of the actors in any scenario, the problem of intentionality must be addressed.

Briefly, there are two arguments that must be considered. The first argument is a vestige of empiricism that claims that because we cannot sensually perceive human intentions, they do not have any scientific significance. For the crude empiricist, arguments over alleged intentionality are invariably "metaphysical." Such crude empiricism is self-contradictory, for those who dispute the existence of intentionality must prove its nonexistence. But this is logically impossible; one can never prove the existence of a negative. Invariably, those who deny intentionality are showing intentionality in the process of disputing its validity. To claim that intentions do not exist is to assail the logical status of one's own (intended) denial.

Any attempt to reduce human intentions to chemical stimuli is subject to the same self-referential problem. People who root intentions solely in physiological and chemical phenomena must recognize their own objections as the product of the same atomistic factors. The self-referential problem is also apparent in those approaches that view human intentions as a mere reflection of social or material forces. This is the basis of vulgar economic determinism.

Both Hayek and Marx have been accused of endorsing the determinist view that people's intentions and motivations are the sole product of social or material factors. While it is possible to interpret their works as variants of determinism, both Hayek and Marx are committed to richer, more integrated modes of analysis. When Hayek argues that people act within a certain sociohistorical context, he does not mean that their intentions are reducible to or purely determined by this context. The context shapes and is shaped by human intentions. It is composed of individual human actors, and is the framework within which social interaction takes place. Hayek's approach posits neither linear causality nor strict determinism; it is *relational*. It recognizes the powers and limitations of the mind by removing it from the realm of pure abstraction, placing it within a concrete social and historical process. This process is both evolutionary and interpersonal. It is beyond people's ability to control directly, even as it shapes their capacity to choose.

Certain versions of Marxism can be criticized also for a tendency toward determinism. These "vulgar" or economistic versions reduce all human intentions to material factors. Yet, as we will see, Marx's doctrine of internal relations—like Hayek's—is not strictly deterministic. It recognizes that human intentions are organically linked to material existence. It does not deny the existence of conscious human purpose. On the contrary, Marx speaks of the primacy of *conscious existence*. He recognizes the dialectical interplay of human intentions and unintended consequences. Such thinkers as Jon Elster and Karl Polanyi have rightfully emphasized this important aspect in Marxian thought that focuses on the unintended social repercussions of nearly all purposeful, human action.[6]

There is a second argument that disputes the scientific significance of intentions and unintended consequences. This psychological argument accepts the existence of human intentions, but it claims that we are unable to state with any degree of certainty exactly what someone's intentions are, since we do not glimpse the inner workings of a person's subconscious mind. Hence, the distinction between intended and unintended consequences is dubious, in this view, because the social scientist can never fully articulate what motivates human action. Since peoples' motives are not directly visible to us, it is conceivable that they may rationalize their actions to disguise their true intentions. People may act in ways that appear opposite from their expressed motivations.

Such a psychologistic argument is irrelevant to the central issue of whether intentional human action generates unintended social consequences. On an introspective level, I am distinctly aware that my own intentions are not always directly translated into a state of affairs that is exactly what I had planned. On a broader level, however, the debate over unintended consequences cannot be reduced to a theory about human psychology or isolated, autonomous human action. The theory is about *social* interaction. In the interpersonal, intertemporal, interspatial realm of social interaction, there is a meshing of motives and plans. A synthesis results, which has greater social significance than any of its isolated individual components. The whole concept of "sociality" has such an affinity with unintended consequences that it is partly constitutive of the phenomenon itself.

If we did consider the psychological realm however, we could find a phenomenon that is similar to the social notion of unintended consequences. It is a well-recognized principle in psychology that emotions are partly the effects of past experiences integrated into the evaluative framework of the mind. For example, when I see a stranger walking down the street, I may become frightened. I may be unaware that I have made a subconscious connection between my visual experience and a certain frightening event in my past. My mind makes split-second, subconscious, relational integrations that lead to a feeling of impending doom. Psychology becomes a potentially radical science because its goal is to get to the root of such emotional upheaval. Perhaps emotions might be considered the spontaneous, unintended consequences of our past—emergent impulses whose origins we may never fully understand, but whose meaning we must seek to articulate. Indeed, this is one of the prime purposes of depth hermeneutics in the Habermasian reconstruction.

In the social sciences and humanities, examples of "order" as a spontaneous, unintended formation abound. The Common Law is a testament to an emergent legality that shows high complexity, sophistication, and flexibility. Customs, values, monetary standards, market relations, and economic systems evolve through generations of commerce, exchange, and social interaction. Language itself, with its rules of grammar and idiom, emerges from communication, which is necessarily interpersonal. None of these social formations was deliberately intended or designed. It is crucially significant, for instance, that the "One-World" language explicitly designed by humans, Esperanto, is not spoken regularly by anyone, except perhaps, by its original inventors in certain isolated instances.

The growth of knowledge itself creates its own spontaneous, evolutionary dynamic. Literature on the subject of evolutionary epistemology is vast. Certain thinkers, such as Popper, Lakatos, Musgrave, Kuhn, and Hacking present an extraordinary consensus on the evolutionary growth of knowledge. Others, like W. W. Bartley, have argued that the affirmation of a theory involves many logical implications that are not immediately apparent to the original theorist. Thus, "the informative content of any idea includes an infinity of unforeseeable non-trivial statements." The creation of mathematics for instance, "generates problems that are wholly independent of the intentions of its creators."[7]

The hermeneutic tradition, too, makes the notion of unintended consequences one of its methodological hallmarks. Paul Ricoeur's classic essay on "The Model of the Text" offers one such illustration. Ricoeur maintains that in the same way that a text is detached from its author, so an action is detached from its agent, developing consequences of its own. Actions are social because they necessarily lead to unintended consequences. Likewise, actions have unintended consequences because they take place within a social context. A meaningful action leaves a trace that goes beyond its relevance to its initial situation, addressing itself to an indefinite range of possible "readers."[8] In hermeneutics, the meaning of the text must be understood in terms of the author's context, and in the context of the multiple interpretations that emerge throughout its evolved history.

Social and economic historians are constantly exploring the unintended social consequences of public policy. Writers as diverse as Milton Friedman, Gabriel Kolko, and Theodore Lowi document the extent to which American government regulatory agencies, allegedly established as a means of protecting the consumer, become the captives of the industries they were meant to regulate. Kolko, for instance, interprets regulation as an outgrowth of explicit industrialist plans to use the state as an instrument of cartelization and stabilization. He suggests, however, that even designed regulations create unintended consequences or side effects that generate demands for greater regulation.

Strangely enough, Hayek agrees with this New Leftist critique of the American Progressive movement. The regulatory dynamic constitutes one of the classic roads to serfdom that Hayek warned against in the 1940s. Hayek wrote that the regulatory process generates internal contradictions in the market that lead to demands for more extensive government regulation. Interventionism seems to embody an inexorable logic toward the establishment of authoritarianism. Similar observations about the progressive income tax serving the rich, or the public housing program contributing to urban blight, or welfare creating dependency are all examples of the social consequences that are often contrary to the expressed intentions of those who have designed and/or supported the initial action.[9]

Constructivist Rationalism versus Critical Rationalism

It seems clearer by example that the conception of emergent social formations as the unintended consequence of human action is not unique to Hayek or to the evolutionist perspective. What is perhaps uniquely Hayekian are the terms he uses to describe the two different forms of rationalism that underlie these divergent theories of social evolution. Hayek argues that the Cartesian rationalists promoted an arrogant conception of reason's power that was blind to the forces of historical evolution. Hayek calls these rationalist thinkers "naive" or "constructivistic."[10] They assume that institutions that benefit mankind have "in the past—and ought in the future to be invented in clear awareness of the desirable effects they produce."[11] Constructivism presumes that people can design (or "construct") social institutions as if they were outside the context of history, using the infinite powers of their reason. Constructivism is the "fatal conceit" endangering the future of wealth, morals, and peace.[12] It is an abuse of reason based on a misconception of its powers, and in the end leads to a destruction of that free interplay of many minds on which the growth of reason nourishes itself.[13]

While Hayek makes reference to Descartes as a constructivist, his writings are curiously deficient in providing examples of other constructivist thinkers. Even where he is most obviously critical of Marx, he fails to consider the significant nonconstructivist elements in Marxian social theory.[14] Typically, Hayek reserves the "constructivist" label for a whole bureaucratic class of twentieth century social engineers.

Hayek contrasts constructivist rationalism with a legitimate alternative, which he calls "critical rationalism."[15] He believes that "reason properly used" is a human faculty that acknowledges its own limited potential. Reason, like other human faculties, is a product of evolution. It is wrong to "suppose that our reason is in a higher critical position and that only those moral rules are valid that reason endorses."[16] Social scientists need to recognize "that order generated without design can far outstrip plans men consciously contrive."[17]

Hayek criticizes socialism for its constructivist attempt to invert the structure of social order. The extended order of human cooperation is the emergent, spontaneous product of social interaction. The contrived order of socialism attempts to rationally design a social system in disregard of the requirements of civilization. But it is virtually impossible, in Hayek's view, to consciously design such order, when order itself is a complex, emergent, organic unity. No central planner can fully comprehend, control, or design the network of myriad interrelationships that generate—and are generated by—the social totality.

The critique of constructivism is deeply relevant to Hayek's view of central planning and utopian theorizing. Hayek's earlier works identify constructivism as an outgrowth of the inappropriate transference of the alleged methods of the physical sciences to the realm of the social sciences. Such "scientism" attempts to deal with social phenomena as if they were subject to precise scientific methods of control, prediction, and experimentation.[18] In later years, however, Hayek noted that his attitudes toward scientism had changed. He learned from Karl Popper that natural scientists did not adhere to the scientistic paradigm that many social scientists tried to imitate.[19]

More recent works by Hayek emphasize that, as an outgrowth of the Cartesian rationalist tradition, constructivism views as unreasonable anything that cannot be "scientifically" proven, validated, or understood. Constructivism rejects those things that lack a fully specified purpose or may generate unknown effects. Its mechanistic approach to human affairs conceives of social order as a form of arrangement and control. Constructivists believe they can gain access to all those facts that may facilitate social engineering. What makes the extended, spontaneous order of capitalism so unappealing to the constructivist mentality is that its social formations are not the products of explicit human design. Constructivism rejects the extended order because it appears both "unreasonable" and "unscientific."[20]

It is perhaps more understandable at this point, just how similar Hayekian insights are to those of the Frankfurt school. The Critical theorists argue, like Hayek, that the researcher was "part of the social object he was attempting to study . . . His perception was mediated through social categories above which he could not rise."[21] Critical theory's opposition to both positivism and the mechanistic conception of reason has a basic similarity to Hayek's critique of constructivism. This is the "instrumentalist" form of reason identified, in the aftermath of World War II, by the Frankfurt school. For these Critical thinkers, instrumentalism applied reason to the realm of technique but not to human values; its ultimate by-product was Auschwitz.

As descendants of the Marxist tradition, the Frankfurt school theorists argued that instrumentalism was historically specific to capitalism. They believed that it would be transcended in socialist society. Likewise, they claimed, socialism would transcend unintended social consequences. It was Jürgen Habermas who attempted to provide a more explicit epistemological foundation for this triumph over unintended consequences. A brief discussion of his resolution appears in Chapter Seven.

Problematic Issues in Hayekian Evolutionism

The Hayekian structure of analysis generates some important questions that should be addressed briefly. Though Hayek offers an epistemological critique of utopianism, he embraces several rather controversial positions concerning social evolution. These positions are not essential to, nor do they affect the substance of, Hayek's critique. But they do suggest weaknesses in Hayek's general social theory.

In keeping with the organic approach of his methodology, Hayek sees evolution as a competition among various traditions. These traditions embody rival rules of action and perception which, through a process of natural selection, determine those rules and institutions that are more durable than others.[22] Ultimately, for Hayek, cultures are successful to the extent that they economize on the amount of articulated knowledge necessary for an individual to function in that society.[23] Societies illustrate their success through their relative increase in population and wealth. As a classical liberal, Hayek values the expanding division of labor, the market, and the common law precisely because they embody discovery procedures within which social learning occurs. But still, Hayek fails to provide a substantive *ethical* defense of the free society.

Hayek does not present a theory of inevitable progress. Yet he sees a close affinity between the spontaneous order of the capitalist market economy and the evolving rules of just conduct. Libertarians may object to the possible "nonlibertarian" consequences of such evolutionism, while Marxists would object to Hayek's "reified" notion of the market as the culmination of social evolution. It seems that Hayek's conclusions do not portend well for the spontaneous emergence of a libertarian, market-oriented social framework.

Norman Barry notes correctly that social evolution has promoted the existence of both liberal and nonliberal institutions. The "free market" and "limited government" are rarities in history. They may "be regarded as perhaps a chance mutation in a course of evolution which is proceeding in quite another direction, an evanescent torch in an inexorably darkening world." In Barry's view, Hayek ties us much too closely to tradition, while seeing reason as "too fragile an instrument to recommend satisfactory alternatives." This suggests that people are incapable of evaluating "critically that statist and anti-individualist order of society which seems to have as much claim to be a product of evolution as any other social structure."[24] On these issues, Barry's arguments are persuasive.

For example, Hayek admits that legislation can correct the "undesirable" consequences of a common law which serves "class" interests. Yet, he does not give an adequate account or definition of power and class relationships. He offers no reason for trusting either the functional adequacy or the class neutrality of the legislature. The libertarian theorist, Murray Rothbard, has criticized Hayek's lack of a class concept. Rothbard shares with Hayek a commitment to Austrian economics, but he argues that the exclusive focus on unintended social consequences "whitewash[es] the growth of government in the 20th century." To view social outcomes as primarily unintended is to assert categorically "that no person or group ever willed the pernicious consequences" of the state's growth. For Rothbard, to stress "the Ferguson-Hayek formula" is to obscure "the self-interested actions" of real human actors.[25] Contemporary theorists on the left criticize Hayek's social theory for reasons that are remarkably similar. For instance, Hilary Wainwright rejects Hayek's emphasis on "accident [as] the main mechanism of social evolution . . ." Despite a "libertarian starting-point," Hayek is apt to favor "bizarre constitutional proposals" in an attempt to bolster the force of tradition.[26]

Hayek's belief that the legislature can correct "undesirable" consequences is also questionable, given his general abdication of the realm of morality to custom. No social scientist—no human being—can escape the necessity to judge. When Hayek argues that "undesirable" consequences can be corrected, he uses an implicit moral standard by which to distinguish the desirable from the undesirable. He alludes to a standard of value without any explicit articulation or rational justification. He eschews such "rationalizations" of morality since, in his opinion, moral customs and traditions are beyond the scope of reason to understand, explain, or construct anew. And yet, without rationally defined moral standards, Hayek's evolutionism can be used to legitimate nearly every existing institutional form. Hence, by virtue of its durability, slavery has as much moral claim to existence as freedom.

There are more fundamental problems with Hayek's social theory. By positing such a sharp distinction between spontaneous and designed order, Hayek has not provided us with any explanation of the emergence of those institutions that are agencies of constructivism. The state is one such agency, and it is the embodiment of all coercive attempts to plan humanity's destiny. To what extent is the state itself a spontaneous, emergent product of social evolution? To what extent does the state define the parameters of the extended order that Hayek celebrates? What are the actual interrelationships between the spontaneous order of the market and the designed institutions of the state? The reader of Hayek's works will strain to find developed answers to any of these important questions.

Hayek's distinction between spontaneous and designed order has certain dualistic overtones. Dualism obscures the *organic* interrelationships between spontaneous and designed orders.[27] A dualistic method overemphasizes the opposition of spontaneity and design, while underemphasizing their historical and developmental unity.

Hayek is adept at tracing the spontaneous emergence of market categories. But he does not offer a similar scenario for the spontaneous evolution of power and class relationships, and state structures. He is apt to make the dualistic claim that "Societies form [spontaneously] but states are made."[28] By viewing the state as a constructivist intrusion on the evolutionary process, Hayek fails to consider the evolutionary development of the state itself.

Hayek's view of social evolution does not provide a clear enough standard by which to distinguish spontaneous institutions from designed organizations. There is a sense in which all institutions are emergent. There is also a sense in which all institutions are designed—some piecemeal, others by constitutional construction. Measuring the effects of each form upon the other, the nature and degree of their interpenetration, the class dynamics of their interrelationships—these are exciting social and historical issues that Hayek has not addressed sufficiently.

None of this is to be construed as an indictment of Hayek's critique of utopianism. The next chapter demonstrates that Hayek's anticonstructivism is as critical of the rationalistic tradition of liberalism as it is of Marxism. Both of these intellectual traditions embody a belief in human perfectibility that, Hayek believes, is epistemologically unjustifiable.

3 Constructivism and Human Efficacy

Hayek's understanding of constructivist rationalism is central to his critique of utopian theorizing. The utopian theorist internalizes a constructivist conception of rationality. But constructivism is a historical product with important psychosocial significance. Hayek recognizes that just as the Western concept of rationality is the product of both Enlightenment thought and market capitalism, so constructivism is an inappropriate extension of the Enlightenment faith in reason.[1] Hayek writes:

> If the Enlightenment has discovered that the role assigned to human reason in intelligent construction had been too small in the past, we are discovering that the task which our age is assigning to the rational construction of new institutions is far too big.[2]

Hayek's reaction against the Enlightenment's reification of reason is much in the spirit of Critical theory. John Caputo suggests that the Critical theorists sought to redefine reason in a way that rescued it from Cartesian constructivism. For the Critical theorists, the Enlightenment subjected reason to the utopian ideal of unconditioned, abstract, ahistorical, noncontextual rationality.[3] By ascribing to people the characteristics of an omniscient deity, and then condemning their reason for not living up to this ideal, constructivist rationalists undermined the legitimacy of cognition.

For Hayek, as for many of his Critical contemporaries, the revolt against constructivist rationalism was not a revolt against reason. Hayek's analysis encompasses both negative and positive moments. In its negative aspects it is a critical reflection on the constructivist distortion of reason. In its positive aspects it comprehends reason as a *human* faculty, one that cannot be abstracted from its contextual specificity.

The Search for Efficacy

Why reason has been so thoroughly abstracted from its context is an issue with deep social and psychological implications. Hayek did not investigate these implications fully, and they are not directly relevant to the validity of his constructivist thesis. Nevertheless, it is useful to provide some insight into the sociopsychological basis of constructivist rationalism.

Constructivism can be seen as a social expression of the human need for psychological efficacy. Butler D. Shaffer writes:

> The critical factor motivating the imposition of structure would appear to stem from a basic need that men have to make the world about them predictable and subject. The maintenance of "orderly" social relationships is an adjunct of man's basic metaphysical need for an environment providing a consistent outcome for his actions.[4]

Shaffer suggests that constructivism is a reified product of abstraction. It is an outgrowth of a selective focus on the apparently limitless capacity of human reason, abstracted from its real context.

The human capacity to know appears infinite, in the sense that the knowledge of one fact presupposes that a person can attain knowledge of a second fact, a third fact, and so on. This knowledge-series can be extended to infinity. But infinity is only a mathematical concept; it is invalid as a concept pertaining to human epistemological potential.[5] A human being, however, is neither immortal nor omniscient. At any point in time, a person's actual knowledge is limited. Constructivism collapses the distinction between actuality and potentiality. It deifies the human ability to know and embraces a concept of reason that transcends human epistemic strictures.

Humans think within a definite structure. Their minds need such structure in order to think. Their sensory apparatus perceives real things and processes in the universe, while their rational faculty apprehends structural and logical interrelationships. They achieve the cognitive efficacy that is requisite to their survival, by acting in accordance with the laws of logic, to produce desired effects.[6] All of natural science is an attempt to systematize human knowledge of consistent and predictable relationships. Science charts certain courses of action initiated by particular entities with distinctive natures, producing specific effects.

In human affairs, however, one person's attempt to generate a desired effect is tempered by the reality of other people who are engaging in similar actions. The result is often a product that no one intended. To a constructivist rationalist, this is incompatible with the human need for predictability and certainty. The constructivist wishes to create a social laboratory in which people are made to act with the same predictability as a cup pushed off a table.

Hayek argues that there are aspects of social reality that are not subject to direct human control. However, unintended consequences are not a sign of human inefficacy; they are a purely social product. Constructivism requires people to step outside the sociohistorical process in order to comprehend and control it. It presumes that people can know all of the facts that animate their existence. It supposes that people can predict every consequence of every action. In essence, it adopts omniscience as the standard of certainty. But omniscience is not a standard for *human* certainty because it is not possible to *human* consciousness. Since "knowledge . . . is not given to anyone in its totality," it is impossible for any person to achieve a synoptic identification of the whole.[7] According to Hayek, such an attempt at omniscience is an abuse of reason.

In Hayek's view a "critical rationalism" is the only antidote to constructivism, because it recognizes the genuine limits—and real potential—of human cognition.[8] For Hayek, the strictures on human knowledge are not merely quantitative; they are qualitative as well. Indeed, "there is . . . a body of very important but unorganized knowledge which cannot possibly be called scientific in the sense of knowledge of general rules . . ." Hayek recognizes "the knowledge of the particular circumstances of time and place" as of utmost importance.[9] He characterizes this epistemic dimension as tacit and practical.

Tacit Knowledge

There are three kinds of rules that Hayek sees as essential to the formation of social order. The first are "rules that are merely observed in fact but have never been stated in words." Hayek gives as an example, the "sense of justice" or "the feeling for language" that refers "to such rules which we are able to apply, but do not know explicitly." The second are "rules that, though they have been stated in words, still merely express approximately what has long been generally observed in action." These first two dimensions are tacit components of knowledge. The third are "rules that have been deliberately introduced and therefore necessarily exist as words set out in sentences." This dimension forms the articulated component of knowledge.[10]

We do not know why certain customs or taboos exist, except that some of them seem to embody an unarticulated "wisdom of the ages." Skills and crafts are passed on for generations without people being able to articulate exactly what they do in their specialty. They may, for instance, "know how" to use a tool, or steer a boat, or play an instrument. But they may not be able to explain the actual creative process, and may not understand the physical or physiological principles involved in the continued reproduction of the skill. Should they come to recognize and articulate such principles, their very definition of the principles incorporates rules of language that guide their thoughts, though they have not explicitly formulated or articulated these rules either. As Hayek observes, "the ability of small children to use language in accordance with rules of grammar and idiom of which they are wholly unaware" is a striking instance of this phenomenon. Hayek quotes Edward Sapir approvingly, who stated in the 1920s that there is

> a far reaching moral in the fact that even a child may speak the most difficult language with idiomatic ease but that it takes an unusually analytical type of mind to define the mere elements of that incredibly subtle linguistic mechanism which is but a plaything in the child's unconscious.[11]

As with language, so with moral values, "man has more often learnt to do the right thing without comprehending why it was the right thing, and he is still more often served by custom than by understanding."[12]

The works of Michael Polanyi deeply influenced Hayek in this area. Polanyi points out that there are two different kinds of awareness that exemplify the difference between "knowing how" to do something and "knowing what" one is doing. They are "subsidiary awareness" and "focal awareness." A pianist may be subsidiarily aware of playing the piano, but not focally aware of the movement of each of his or her fingers.

> If a pianist shifts his attention from the piece he is playing to the observation of what he is doing with his fingers while playing it, he gets confused and may have to stop. This happens

generally if we switch our focal attention to particulars of
which we had previously been aware only in their subsidiary
role.[13]

Practical skills and habits, customs of thought and action are
instances of knowing how to do something without necessarily being
aware of exactly what we are doing. Hayek explains:

> Men may "know how" to act, and the manner of their action
> may be correctly described by an articulated rule, without their
> explicitly "knowing that" the rule is such and such. Of course,
> once particular articulations of rules of conduct have become
> accepted, they will be the chief means of transmitting such
> rules; and the development of articulated and unarticulated
> rules will constantly interact.[14]

Hayek shows a keen awareness of the dialectical interrelationship between articulated and unarticulated social practices and
knowledge. These two dimensions interact in ways that propel people toward a deeper understanding of themselves and of the world
around them. However, Polanyi emphasizes that even as we articulate rules, our definitions can only reduce and shift "the tacit coefficient of meaning" but they cannot entirely eliminate it.[15] Even
though our knowledge of our past, our customs, and our values have
evolved and grown, Polanyi suggests that the dynamic process is
unending. We may "remain ever unable to say all that we know" just
as "we can never quite know what is implied in what we say."

The tacit dimension of knowledge, embodied in skills, customs, and traditions, is part of the rich fabric of social reality that
may partially explain why human actions generate unintended social
consequences. If we are not entirely aware of the reasons for, or the
context of our actions, we will never be able to ascertain their exact
repercussions. Of course, it is also true that even if all knowledge
could be articulated, there would still be unintended social consequences precisely because people do not know the state and content of each other's knowledge and, thus, cannot predict the outcomes of every action.[16]

Thus, for Hayek, utopian constructivism could not possibly
transcend the unintended consequences of all social action. The
utopian attempt to entirely redesign society presumes an omniscient
grasp of every constituent element in the network of a social whole.
Utopian constructivism would require full knowledge not only of

quantifiable and articulated forms, but of practical elements, social and individual, which were predominantly tacit and experiential in nature. Ultimately, totalistic, utopian blueprints for social change rest on what Hayek describes as a "synoptic delusion."[17]

The Synoptic Delusion

A synoptic delusion represents a false belief that one can consciously design a new society as if one had possession of holistic knowledge. Holistic knowledge involves grasping the complex interrelations of the society that are necessarily constituted by both articulate and inarticulate social practices. At the risk of trivializing an important fact, we can safely assume that Hayek has provided new insight into human fallibility. People create pencils with erasers and typewriters with correction fluid because they make mistakes. Omniscience implies that humans are not fallible. They would even have to acquire knowledge of the structure and processes of their own mind. Hayek observes:

> There will always be some rules governing a mind which that mind in its then prevailing state cannot communicate, and that, if it ever were to acquire the capacity of communicating these rules, this would presuppose that it had acquired further higher rules which make the communication of the former possible but which themselves will still be incommunicable.[18]

Thus, Hayek believes that the idea of a mind explaining itself is a logical contradiction. Its impossibility gives us a lesson in cognitive humility, curbing our intellectual hubris.[19]

Hayek extends this principle into the social realm. Just as the mind is limited in its ability to articulate the rules of its own operation, so too are individuals limited in their ability to articulate the rules on which social order depends.[20] Human fallibility, and the inherent, contextual limits of human knowledge, are then the strongest factors militating against a fully imposed or designed utopian order. The attempted imposition of order dislocates the very processes that make order possible. For Hayek utopianism rests on "proposals for the improvement of undesirable effects of the existing system, based upon a complete disregard of those forces which actually enabled it to work."[21] By severing the connection between goals and context, actions and conditions, utopians are unable to implement their detailed blueprints for an ideal society.

It has been noted that Hayek's opposition to a fully imposed or designed order is a commentary on something that has never existed and could never exist. This is why the critique applies to *utopian* theory. Nevertheless, Hayek is susceptible to the criticism that his approach is "vacuous . . . except as a polemic against Utopian fantasies," because it does not examine the wide range of social and economic institutions that combine elements of planning and spontaneity.[22] The crucial choice in contemporary social policy is not between a fully emergent and a fully designed order, but between degrees of each.

Realistically, the issue of emergent versus designed order is one that compels an answer to the question: How much design is possible? Even a thorough Idealist such as Blanshard has argued that the question of degrees is essential. In examining an organic system in which everything is related to everything else, one must focus "on certain factors selectively and to the exclusion of others," or else "science would seem to be one great blunder." Indeed, Blanshard argues, "relevance has degrees."[23] Though we are not omniscient, "we *can* have *some* knowledge without an exhaustive grasp of relations."[24] How much knowledge—and how much design—is possible?

Ultimately this is the central epistemic issue distinguishing Marx from Hayek. While Marx views history as the mechanism of resolution, Hayek believes that social change can occur only through a tinkering with the rules of just conduct. These rules cannot be wholly overturned for they are the emergent historical and cultural products of evolution. For Hayek, such rules embody a tacit component that is not, and perhaps cannot be, articulated.

Furthermore, Hayek gives us little reason to trust the functional adequacy or class neutrality of any legislative group that tinkers with these emergent principles. He gives us no way to evaluate objectively the need for such correction other than a process of "muddling through" the sociocultural whole and judging its components in terms that are immanent, that is, specific and internal to a given society. Therefore, if a society values slavery, there is no objective standard by which to condemn, or alter, its existence. Morals, in the Hayekian framework, are not a matter of choice. They are culturally transmitted and, often, tacitly accepted. Hayekian evolutionism does not offer any adequate prescription for these important normative questions.

But if the critique of utopianism is a critique of something that has never existed, then the crucial question is whether or not Hayek

is attacking "strawmen." If utopianism is made to look so intellectually unattractive, how can any rational thinker endorse its
premises?

For Hayek the danger of epistemic utopianism is not that it is
implementable. The danger lies in the actions of modern statist
social engineers who impose their designs on a social totality *as if*
they possessed holistic knowledge. In Hayek's view, the central planners and bureaucrats wreak havoc on the economies they seek to
control precisely because no person can possibly grasp the sophisticated complexities of the organic social whole. Just as the reified
conception of reason has been used by intellectual constructivists to
attack the legitimacy of genuinely *human* cognition, so too, the presumption of omniscience has allowed central planners to attack the
legitimacy of spontaneously emergent social institutions. These
social engineers can never achieve holistic knowledge, because
knowledge, as such, is both articulate and tacit, and essentially dispersed among the many individual actors who comprise the social
totality.

Thus, for Hayek, utopianism, as a fallacious epistemological
doctrine, is the basis of instrumentalist, state-guided, centralized
planning. Utopianism perpetuates a polarity between its detailed
visions for the ideal society and the existential conditions it ignores.
It severs the internal relationship between theorists and their context. Its proposals for a new society are constructed in an abstract
manner, external to the sociohistorical process. In attempting to
bridge the gap between theory and practice, it demands that all
human actors adhere to a noncontextual, ahistorical model.
Inevitably, utopians embrace social engineering as their prime mode
of political action. Ignoring organic, social interrelationships, the
utopian attempt to actualize the ideal must generate dystopian, unintended social consequences.

It would be a mistake to assume that Hayek's critique applies
only to utopian, socialistic planning. The Hayekian critique of utopia
is as much an indictment of rationalistic liberalism as it is of modern-day socialism. In his defense of the extended, spontaneous order,
Hayek recognizes that the movement toward capitalism "requires a
very slow and gradual change in national morals and national customs, which takes a few generations." Without such an evolutionary
change, the market economy is "bound to fail."[25] Hayek denies validity to an abstract, universalized, transhistorical conception of natural rights as a philosophical justification for capitalism. No one can
gain such a transcendent view of the world and construct principles

that are universally appropriate for all contexts. Rules and morals are emergent. In this sense, even the conception of natural rights is emergent, perhaps, an undeniably important expression of a liberal society's concern for justice. But for Hayek, the doctrine of natural rights is a constructivist device that attempts to represent the immense complexity of law in the simple Lockean maxims of self-ownership and nonaggression.

Though Hayek denies its validity, he appreciates the moral vision of the natural rights perspective. Yet Hayek admits that he knows

> of no way of preventing coercion altogether and that all we can hope to achieve is to minimize it or rather its harmful effects. The sad fact is that nobody has yet found a way in which the former can be achieved by deliberate action. Such a happy state of perfect freedom (as I should call it) might conceivably be attained in a society whose members strictly observed a moral code prohibiting all coercion. Until we know how we can produce such a state, all we can hope is to create conditions in which people are prevented from coercing each other.[26]

It is supremely Hayekian for Hayek to admit his ignorance. It is also supremely Hayekian to admit that certain limits on our knowledge are historically specific. Someday, perhaps, we may know how to produce a law code that is relevant to its context and expressive of a genuine cultural appreciation for the morality of nonaggression. Until then, Hayek claims, the advocates of natural rights have embraced a utopian method of translating liberal theory into social reality. It is utopian because it seeks to design a society based on rules of just conduct that nobody has the power to make effective.

Hayek's rejection of rationalistic liberalism and modern-day socialist planning is not an outright dismissal of Marxism. But Marx's response to the Hayekian worldview is paradoxical. Marx's historical resolution provides an alleged mechanism through which a greater degree of designed order can emerge spontaneously. This designed order is not a totalitarian imposition. For Marx, it reflects the triumph of human efficacy on a social scale. People are no longer the playthings of blind historical forces; they conquer the polarity between conscious human purpose and unintended social consequences.

Marx agrees with the Hayekian approach in its assertion that criticism of social institutions is immanent. To the extent that people seek to change society, their goals must be consistent and compatible with the context from which they spring. But whereas Hayek recognizes certain transhistorical, epistemic strictures, Marx suggests that these limits are historically specific to capitalism. By changing the conditions of human existence, Marx seeks to overcome the historical limitations of human knowledge. Marx believes that in the communist utopia human reason will be able to generate the desired social effects. His resolution is the subject of Part Two.

It must be emphasized at this juncture, however, that Hayek's critique of utopianism is not a rejection of the radical project. Radicalism must incorporate the evolutionist concern for historical and social context, while embracing a progressive view of human peace, freedom, and dignity. But there is a conservative tendency within the evolutionist approach that views the critique of utopianism as a renunciation of *radicalism*. This conviction is gravely mistaken.

In *The Open Society and Its Enemies*, for instance, Popper equates utopian "reconstruction" with "radicalism." Popper argues that irrationalism "is inherent in radicalism. It is not reasonable to assume that a complete reconstruction of our social world would lead at once to a workable system." For Popper, "The canvas cleaning can be sweeping and violent," leading people to replace reason by "a desperate hope for political miracles." Despite the radicals' "intoxication with dreams of a beautiful world," they only succeed in creating a hell on earth, "that hell which man alone prepares for his fellow men."[27]

Hayek rejects Popper's denigration of radicalism. A truly radical project does not aim for a clean, ahistorical social slate. By equating radicalism and utopianism, Popper attacks the analytical integrity of genuinely radical social theory. By contrast, Hayek argues that "we are bound all the time to question fundamentals." This is the essence of a radical approach. Yet, "while it must be our privilege to be radical, this ought not to mean 'advanced' in the sense that we claim to know which is the only forward direction."[28] Any approach that deserves this privileged distinction must take full account of Hayekian strictures.

Though Hayek defends radicalism against Popperian conservatism, it is also true that his moral agnosticism has profound conservative ramifications, as Barry suggests. Social evolution does not necessarily culminate in Hayek's neoliberal vision. Clearly, much more work needs to be done within the neoliberal academy to articulate a genuinely libertarian radicalism, one that is critical and revolutionary, but neither Marxist in its substantive orientation nor conservative in its political implications.[29]

The value of Hayek's framework lies in his suggestion that genuine radicals must defend reason "against its abuse by those who do not understand the conditions of its effective functioning and continuous growth."[30] His critique of constructivism and utopianism is simultaneously a tribute to partially knowing social actors, whose efficacious use of *human* reason cannot be abstracted from the concrete specificity of context.

PART TWO

Marx and the Epistemic Utopia

4   Capitalism and Dualism

Having examined the Hayekian critique of utopianism, we now turn to the similarly dialectical analysis of Karl Marx. In order to grasp the full implications of Marx's critique, however, it is useful to view his project as a response to dualism. Marx's critique of dualism forms the core of his opposition to utopianism, anarchism, and liberalism. His project is as fundamentally opposed to constructivism as anything Hayek has to offer.

The Marxian Critique of Constructivism

Throughout Marx's writings, there is a persistent denigration of those liberal thinkers who view the capitalist system as a logical derivative of the "eternal laws of nature and of reason."[1] The "Robinsonades," as Marx calls them, dissolve society "into a world of atomistic, mutually hostile individuals," who are self-interested and isolated from one another.[2] Whether he was commenting on John Locke or Adam Smith, Marx argued that the liberal vision of civil society as "natural" and "normal" was typical of each epoch in its quest for transhistorical legitimacy.[3] Marx condemns this vision as a product of "vulgar economy" and "bourgeois narrow-mindedness," since liberal thinkers were defending "in doctrinaire fashion" those categories of explanation that were historically specific to the capitalist mode of production.[4]

For Marx, political economy expressed bourgeois social relations as a given, without grasping their historical genesis or transitory quality. Marx views the method of bourgeois political economy as one-dimensional and abstract. As Ollman observes

> An "abstraction" is a part of the whole whose ties with the rest are not apparent; it is a part which *appears* to be a whole in itself.[5]

Marx argues that bourgeois economists abstract from the capitalist system the apparent reciprocity of exchange relations, failing to grasp the essential exploitative character of capitalist production. This emphasis on abstract equality-in-exchange masks the capitalist's extraction of surplus value from the labor process. By focusing on the principle of equality, the liberal economists mistake the part for the whole, reifying the exchange relation as the animating principle of all aspects of the capitalist system.

Thus, Marx claims to identify one of the key dualistic distinctions in capitalism, which he describes as a dichotomy between appearance and essence. The hallmark of bourgeois ideology is the one-dimensional emphasis on appearance. This emphasis was not merely the tool of bourgeois ideologists, according to Marx. It was equally the tool of those utopian and "vulgar" socialists who, like Proudhon, see history as a concretization of "immortal, unchangeable, immutable" principles of Truth, Justice, and Reason.[6] Marx believes that the emphasis on Reason shows a deep "*dualism* between life and ideas, between soul and body, a dualism which recurs in many forms."[7] Such an abstract category is disconnected from the historical specificity that gives it meaning.

Frederick Engels makes the astute observation that an emphasis on the primacy of abstraction is the cornerstone of what he calls, a priori methodology. Engels's critique of Eugen Dühring, reads like a Marxist indictment of constructivist rationalism. Beginning from false axiomatic premises, Dühring formulates a basic moral principle that two human wills are fundamentally equal, and that no person can demand anything positive of another person. Dühring believes that the initiation of force gives rise to a state of injustice. Engels argues that Dühring ascertains the properties of a just social system by logically deducing them from a purely conceived concept of that social system, and then, measuring the reality against the abstraction. This is the essence of utopian theoretical system-building. Engels writes:

> To construct [principles] in one's head, take them as the basis from which to start, and then reconstruct the world from them in one's head is *ideology* . . . The world clearly constitutes a single system, i.e., a coherent whole, but the knowledge of this system presupposes a knowledge of *all* nature and history, which man will *never* attain. Hence he who makes systems must fill in the countless gaps with *figments of his own imagination*, i.e., engage in *irrational* fancies, ideologise.[8]

System-building comprehends certain truths, while abstract-ing these from the context within which they are concretely mani-fested. The utopian may assert correctly that all the aspects of social reality are interdependent, and hence, in need of restructuring. Yet this abstract interdependence makes it impossible to examine the constituent parts of the whole without taking into account all exist-ing parts. Ultimately, a utopian attempt at system-building depends on a doctrine of strict organicity and the omniscience this implies. Like Hayek, both Marx and Engels reject this approach uncondi-tionally.

The danger of abstract system-building lies in the ideological nature of the enterprise. Engels argues that the attempt to elaborate an "all-comprising system" often degenerates into an exercise in metaphysical argument, such "that both the first principles of logic and the fundamental laws of the universe had existed from all eter-nity for no other purpose than to ultimately lead to this newly-dis-covered, crowning theory."[9]

Marx and Engels condemn this unscientific a priori methodol-ogy as the basis of most utopian socialist, bourgeois, and anarchist ideologies. Utopian socialists such as Saint-Simon, Fourier, Owen, Weitling, and Cabet believed that their abstract moral principles would serve as the basis for an ideal socialist commonwealth. Their constructions were external to historical conditions, according to Marx, in disregard of the necessity for class struggle. Generally, the utopians wished to establish socialism instrumentally, by relying on the existing state, regardless of its functional efficiency or class character.[10]

Plamenatz notes correctly that for Marx, the utopians' sweep-ing proposals for change had several pitfalls. First, they depended on "men of goodwill" to actualize their ideal models. They implored people to change their lives on an individual basis, through moral suasion. Second, their unrealistic proposals disregarded both actual existing conditions and potential social consequences. For Marx, the utopians could not implement such ideals by the methods that they adopted.[11]

Unlike the utopian socialists, bourgeois political economists defended market institutions. Inspired by the works of Adam Smith, they accepted a dualistic distinction between civil society and the state. They viewed the state as an external framework for market processes, and divorced the private interests of the individual from the public interests of the citizen. But for Marx and Engels, both utopian socialists and bourgeois ideologists achieved a similarly fractured conception of the social totality. They reified contemporary institutions as transhistorical constancies, and failed to comprehend the organic, structural unity and historical specificity of the capitalist mode of production.

Marx reserved some of his most virulent attacks for such anarchists and libertarian socialists as Bakunin, Godwin, Proudhon, and Stirner. These thinkers utilized their voluntarist moral principles to delegitimate the coercive state and to justify cooperative social institutions. For Marx, such a petit bourgeois approach was entirely dependent on a dualistic conception of the social totality. Marx never conceived of the state as external to the market. He viewed both social formations as *internal* to the capitalist mode of production. "State influences" were outgrowths of capitalism's development, dissolution, and inevitable defeat. Marx argued that in modern political economy, capitalism was never free of state intervention, and hence, never existed in its purest form.[12] In reality, "there exists only approximation; but, this approximation is the greater, the more developed the capitalist mode of production and the less it is adulterated and amalgamated with survivals of former economic conditions."[13]

Paul Thomas observes correctly that for Marx, statism and anarchism, "like blind obedience and blind destruction—have in common a certain specific form of false consciousness." They "are opposite sides of the same idolatrous coin."[14] Thomas argues that the anarchist alternative conceives of freedom and authority as polar opposites, two "independent co-equal principles" that exist in logical—rather than relational—contradiction to one another.[15] Marcuse notes similarly that when this division

> is undertaken dualistically, the world is split in half: two relatively self-enclosed spheres are set up and freedom and unfreedom as totalities divided between them in such a way that one sphere is wholly a realm of freedom and the other wholly a realm of unfreedom.[16]

In Marx's view aspects of anarchism and statism exist side-by-side in organic conjunction. Capitalism, for Marx, merges "anarchy in the social division of labour and despotism in that of the workshop" where these principles "are mutual conditions the one of the other."[17] Socialism will resolve the conflict by transcending both anarchy and despotism, by subjecting the social production process to conscious human control, and by freeing the worker from the "exploitative" control of capital. Marx envisions the full flowering of the human potential, and of the efficacious, integrated human personality.

Marx argues that human liberation could not emerge out of first principles, but only "from a critical knowledge of the historical movement," one "which itself produces the *material conditions of emancipation*." Marx and Engels vehemently opposed a priori methodology.[18] Such was the basis of utopian theory in all of its incarnations. In attempting to write "doctrinaire recipe[s] . . . for the cookshops of the future," utopians were doomed to fail.[19]

The utopians, the bourgeois political economists, and the anarchists were each prisoners of the social and economic categories that they employed.[20] The utopians viewed human liberation in "idealistic" terms, endorsing the "modern mythology" of bourgeois rights and liberties.[21] Libertarian rights, according to Marx, were based on a dualistic distinction between form and content. They sanctioned the form of liberation—free human choice—by abstracting it from the content, that is, the context within which choices are made. Thus, bourgeois "freedom of conscience" merely tolerates religion, rather than liberating the human soul "from the witchery of religion."[22] For Marx, people create religion as the "heart of a heartless world." They will not transcend mysticism until they abandon *"a condition which requires illusions."*[23] Thus, in civil society,

> man was not freed from religion; he received religious freedom. He was not freed from property. He received freedom of property. He was not freed from the egoism of trade, but received freedom to trade.[24]

According to Marx, libertarian rights give material expression to this distinction between form and content. The rights of people are the rights of atomistic people, of people as separate from other people. Private property sanctions this separateness. It defines the limits within which human beings can enjoy their own possessions, seeing "in other men not the *realization* but rather the limitation of [their] own freedom."[25] Bourgeois freedom allows people the abstract right to use and dispose of material possessions in a way that reduces other people to means. It reduces the actor "himself to a means" making him "the plaything of alien powers."

Marx views capitalism as a system that generates a "dualism between individual life and species-life, between the life of civil society and political life."[26] Capitalism cannot resolve the dualities it engenders. It is a social system that relies on spontaneously grown social practices that cannot prevent "the most severe collisions" between hostile spheres of social reality.[27] This spontaneous order generates another, more basic dichotomy between human intentions and unintended social consequences.

The Hayekian perspective suggests that constructivism is an illegitimate expression of the human need for efficacy. Such efficacy entails people's conviction that they are competent to perform the tasks before them. According to Marx, it is capitalism that robs humanity precisely of this competence. The labor process stunts the development of an integrated human being. It is the material expression of a profound dualism, one which not only separates body from mind, and product from producer, but creates an antagonistic distinction between them.

Marx argues that only a revolutionary proletariat can transcend unintended social consequences, while consciously creating nonexploitative social conditions that emerge from specific historical circumstances. Marx projects an extension of the concept of human efficacy, by ascribing to the collective the facility to translate conscious plans into social action with fully determined effects. As we shall see, this attempt to transcend the pitfalls of utopian constructivism relies on a problematic historical resolution.

Nonetheless, Marx was fully cognizant of the limits of reason. He criticizes utopians for their belief that people can achieve collective competence instantaneously. For Marx, such collective competence emerges through historical action, not through constructivist plans based on contrived premises. This is at root Marx's major objection to utopian thought. Marx and Engels argue that for utopian thinkers,

> Historical action is to yield to their personal inventive action, historically created conditions of emancipation to fantastic ones, and the gradually spontaneous class-organisation of the proletariat to an organisation of society *specially* contrived by these inventors. Future history resolves itself, in their eyes, into the propaganda and the practical carrying out of their social plans.[28]

The utopians then, are constructivists, claiming an ability to direct social order that is well beyond their competence. Engels argues further, that the utopians have logically deduced solutions from abstract principles not based on material or historical factors and conditions. For the utopian, society's "wrongs" can only be corrected through reason which enables one

> to discover a new and more perfect system of social order and to impose this upon society from without by propaganda, and, wherever it was possible, by the example of model expressions. These new social systems were foredoomed as utopian; the more completely they were worked out in detail, the more they could not avoid drifting off into pure fantasies.[29]

As Lichtheim suggests, this Marxian rejection of utopian idealism was a recognition of the "poverty of philosophy" divorced from material conditions. Philosophy could not alter society "simply by holding up a scheme of perfection or a conceptual image of 'true' reality . . ." It required an appropriate historical context and a class whose very existence portends the dissolution of the capitalist mode of production.[30]

Marx's view of the utopian as a social engineer seeking to impose a paradigm for perfection on an unsuspecting populace, shares much in common with the Hayekian and Popperian notion of the "canvas cleaner," who attempts to wipe out existing society in disregard of existential and historical conditions. There is a convergence of critique here that cannot be underemphasized.

However, the evidence suggests that Marx and Engels might have rejected the methods of modern social engineers, those statist "utopians" of the former Communist bloc who, without the material prerequisites, attempted unsuccessfully to build socialism on the foundation of quasi-feudalism. Both Marx and Engels might have seen the failure of contemporary Communism as inevitable. They understood that "canvas cleaning" must necessarily wipe out the artist who wishes to start anew. In an original statement of the dangers of constructivism that rivals Burke, Popper, and Hayek for its insight, Engels writes: "Once the spark has been put to the powder . . . the people who laid the spark to the mine will be swept along by the explosion, which will be a thousand times as strong as they themselves." Thus, the revolutionaries are robbed

> of their illusions . . . People who boasted that they *made* a revolution have always seen the day after that they had no idea what they were doing, that the revolution *made* did not in the least resemble the one they intended to make. This is what Hegel calls "the irony of history."[31]

Marx and Engels do not deny that individuals make history. History itself is constituted by human interaction.[32] They agree with Hayek's observation that history is the product of human action but not of deliberate human design. The historical process emerges out of the "conflicts between many individual wills," says Engels, "and what emerges is something that no one intended."[33] Often, the consequences are not merely unforeseeable, but entirely different—or opposite—from the original intentions of the actors.[34]

This recognition of unintended social consequences was one of the defining characteristics of Marx's approach to the social sciences. Elster argues persuasively that Marx was a genuine "pioneer in the use of this methodology."[35] Marx saw the distinction between human intentions and unintended consequences as a prime example of "social contradiction." It was a "perverse" social dualism in which the rational behavior of many individuals generated effects that were disastrous for the society as a whole. Explaining the structure of these unintended social consequences became one of Marx's most important theoretical preoccupations, and was, in Elster's estimation, Marx's "most important methodological achievement."[36]

A Note on Marx and Scottish Liberalism

This preoccupation with unintended social consequences provides us with additional parallels between the Hayekian and Marxian perspectives. Such a theoretical and methodological convergence is hardly surprising. Hayek's approach is deeply rooted in the Scottish Enlightenment. Ronald Meek maintains that this very same Scottish Historical School, of which Adam Smith, Adam Ferguson, William Robertson, and John Millar were a significant part, had a profound impact not only on Marx's critique of political economy, but on Marxist sociology as well. These Scottish thinkers pioneered a materialist conception of history that emphasized the spontaneous emergence of a wide variety of social phenomena. Adam Smith, not unlike Marx, had developed a broad theoretical system that encompassed history, political economy, and moral philosophy.[37] Marx inherited this legacy. He drew explicitly on the evolutionist insights of the Scottish Enlightenment in an attempt to transcend its historical limitations.

Predating Marx, Engels, and Hayek, the Scottish thinkers moved toward a more integrated understanding of the individual as a constituent part of an organic, social whole. While they appreciated the advancing rationality of capitalist production, they also empha-sized the nonrational traditions and customs that molded social behavior. In their recognition of the individualistic quality of bour-geois life, there was a simultaneous recognition of its spontaneous, emergent, social institutions. To this extent, the Scottish thinkers never embraced atomistic individualism.

Despite their common Scottish roots, Marx and Hayek exhibit important differences. While Marx accepts the existence of unin-tended social consequences, a methodological hallmark of Scottish-Burkean-Hayekian thought, he does not believe that it is the per-manent condition of mankind. Richard Flacks, summarizing the Marxian argument, emphasizes that any theory that focuses purely on unintended social consequences qualifies as "ideology." Such a one-dimensional view of human history provides a clue as to "the real nature of social relationships at the time such ideas take root."[38] For Marxists, this view reifies the distinctive characteristics of cap-italism (and all precapitalist social formations). Marx would have criticized Hayek's focus on transhistorical, unintended social con-sequences, since, in his view, they are historically specific to pre-communist epochs. In the Marxian project, true human history does not begin until people have conquered the unintended consequences of their actions.

Marx argues that while capitalism is beyond conscious human agency, its spontaneous order is a historic product of a specific phase of social development. For Marx, this "is precisely the beauty and greatness of" the market. Capitalism's "spontaneous interconnec-tion" reflects a society that is independent of individual wills while presupposing "their reciprocal independence and indifference." Cap-italism's impersonal market forces offer an "objective connection" that is superior to all previous modes of production.[39] In its "anar-chy," in the totality of its "disorderly movement, is to be found its order."[40] But in their orderly social existence, individuals in capital-ism enter into social relations that are independent of their will. Their interactive collisions produce an *alien* social power that stands above them.[41]

Thus far, I have discussed three polarities in Marx's critique of capitalism. The first, a polarity between appearance and essence, is the basis of capitalist ideology. The second, a polarity between form and content, is the foundation of the bourgeois notion of free-dom. The third, a polarity between human intentions and unin-tended social consequences, illustrates the spontaneous character of capitalism, a system that denies to people the ability to master their own fate. From these dualities, Marx claims to identify the existence of more concrete polarities generated by the capitalist mode of production.

Capitalism and Social Fragmentation

Marx observes that capitalism leads to an "infinite fragmentation of means of production, and isolation of the producers themselves."[42] At the foundation of capitalist production is its "first historical presupposition"; Marx identifies this as the separation of "the worker from the conditions of labour, which confront him as independent forces."[43] Whereas in previous modes of production laborers unite within themselves multiple functions, the development of the forces of production leads to a corresponding differentiation in the relations of production. The division of labor is the crucial turning point. Products are no longer the result of individual labor; they are social products produced by the cooperation and combination of many laborers, each of whom performs a different task.[44]

Social labor in capitalism develops out of differentiation and fragmentation. Engels notes that there are three great social divisions of labor that have emerged in historical development. The first is the formation of pastoral tribes from the general masses. The second involves a differentiation of manufacture from agriculture and the corresponding geographic differentiation between town and country. Finally, there emerges a class of merchants who are not laborers and do not produce use-values. The merchants exist to facilitate exchange and as such, they are crucial to capitalist development and expansion.[45]

This division of labor is not a designed social development. It is a spontaneous by-product of social interaction that "continues to grow behind the backs of the producers."[46] Previously combined branches of production become separated, even as each branch internally differentiates its own operations.[47] In capitalist commodity production, "*separation* appears as the normal relation."[48]

Manufacture differentiates the instruments of labor in two ways. Marx describes the first form as "heterogeneous" where the product is created by the mechanical "fitting together" of various partial products that are produced independently of each other. The second form is a "series" where the product is created by a series of interconnected and united processes. The manufacturing process, whether it is heterogeneous or a series, develops the natural endowments of the laborer in a one-sided fashion. The laborer becomes a perfectionist in his or her limited tasks and one-sided specialties. The spontaneous division of labor becomes the "methodical and systematic form of capitalist production."[49]

The division is composed of a dual dynamic. First, according to Marx, it cripples the laborer by pitting the functions of body against the functions of mind. The organic unity of body and mind is fractured, as the laborer's particularized, mechanical abilities are developed to the detriment of cognitive, creative abilities. Second, it expresses the basic alienation of the laborers who become estranged from the product of their labor as they are forced to sell that product, and their own labor-power as a product, on the market.

The market itself exists by virtue of the distinction between the product and the producer, and the distinction between knowledge and labor. The laborer's product becomes externalized and objectified. The early Marx focuses on this process as one "of self-sacrifice," and "mortification." Alienated labor becomes the concretized manifestation of the dualism between product and producer.[50] The later Marx focuses on this alienation as it appears on the market. Marx criticizes the liberal economists who overlook the alienated labor-power that is embodied in exchanged commodities, and who view the social relations of individuals as a relation between things.[51]

The spontaneously developing differences that emerge from this internalized and externalized division and fragmentation of labor lead to the mutual exchanging of products as commodities. On the market dualism takes the form of a division between purchase and sale or the exchange of commodities for money and the exchange of money for commodities. With this functional division in exchange "into two spatially and temporally independent acts," Marx observes the emergence of another dualistic distinction in which "the overall movement of exchange itself become[s] separate from the exchangers, the producers of commodities." The exchange relationship is another sign of unintended social consequences writ large, of how the market in exchange becomes a power that is "external to and independent of the producers," dominating their lives and eluding their conscious control.[52] Money itself, spontaneously emergent in precapitalist society, comes to dominate bourgeois life.

The separation of purchase and sale highlights their polar functions as well as their intrinsic unity. This separation makes possible buying without selling, or commodity stock-piling, and selling without buying, or money accumulation.[53] Speculation and capitalist economic crises are the inevitable outgrowths of this separation.

Marx recognizes that the development of exchange is a chief means for the individuation of human society. "It makes the herd-like existence superfluous and dissolves it."[54] But its progressive character is subverted because capitalism robs people of the ability to consciously plan their own fate. The emergence of more substantive notions of human freedom is coupled with

> the most complete suspension of all individual freedom, and the most complete subjugation of individuality under social conditions which assume the form of objective powers, even of overpowering objects—of things independent of the relations among individuals themselves.[55]

Marx argues too, that there is a fundamental distinction that exists between the proletariat and the capitalist class. This polarity is, of course, central to Marx's interpretation of history as the history of class struggle. Capitalism, according to Marx, creates social conditions in which the property-owning class is able to exploit the propertyless class. This exploitation is a direct outgrowth of the separation of the product from the producer. In the production process, the propertyless laborer endows the product with its value and receives in return only enough for his or her own subsistence. The extraction of surplus value makes possible capitalist accumulation. It is also the material essence of what Marx likes to call capitalist exploitation. It is a manifestation of the dualism between social production and private appropriation.

Despite the exploitative nature of the capital-labor relationship, Marx argues that capitalists themselves engage in a competitive market process over which they too have no control. Capitalists are victims of the same alien social forces. Marx would agree with Hayek's contention that "capitalists who are suspected of directing it all are actually also tools of an impersonal process, just as unaware of the ultimate effects and purpose of their actions."[56] For Marx, capitalist exploitation of workers is not a premeditated plot, but a spontaneous outgrowth of capitalism and its class nature.

In a sense, however, capitalism transcends the prebourgeois dualism between caste and class. As Draper explains, a caste is characterized by fixed, recognized boundaries, while a class is a broader socio-politico-economic category.[57] For Marx, capitalism is a fully developed class society. Class is a relationship to the means of production primarily, but it includes a host of extra-economic structures.

For Marx dualistic distinctions between appearance and essence, form and content, are class expressions. By accentuating the formal equality of capitalist exchange or the formal freedom of bourgeois rights, liberal thinkers, according to Marx, mask the actual domination of the capitalist class and the limited, one-dimensional character of bourgeois liberties. By accentuating the predominance of spontaneous order, liberal thinkers, like Hayek, reify the capitalist reality into a transhistorical abstraction that denies the potential for a genuinely efficacious social existence.

The division and fragmentation of labor, production, and exchange pits individuals against one another, blocking for a time the development of a consolidated proletarian class movement. Yet, if the division in capitalism is responsible for quelling the proletarian revolt, it is also true that the capitalist state, with its monopoly on the coercive use of force, is just as responsible for the oppression of the working class.

The state is not merely an instrument of the capitalist class. Marx's conception is not one of pure conspiracy. The distinction between state and civil society is, according to Marx, another polarity that is historically specific to capitalism. For Marx, the state exists *only* in contrast to civil society.[58] It is out of the "contradiction between the interest of the individual and that of the community [that] the latter takes an independent form as the *state*."[59] The state is not a communal entity, symbolic of abstract will, nor is it Reason personified, as Hegel would have it. The state is divorced from both the real interests of the individual and the society, forming an "illusory community."[60] It gives the illusion of collective purpose in a society fractured by capitalist competition and atomistic divisiveness.

Just as there is fragmentation between state and civil society, so there is a distinction between the democratic form of the liberal state and its class content. Marx identifies different state forms throughout history and within capitalist development. He claims that communism goes beyond the merely formal equality and democracy of bourgeois society, embracing a real community of substantive equality, transcending both civil society and state.

Marx argues too, that there is another crucial dualism in capitalist society, between ideas and reality. In philosophy it is expressed as a split between abstract idealism and mechanical materialism. Idealism, on the one hand, traces the primacy of ideas in history. These ideas, torn from their historical and social context, become disembodied abstractions that mask their class character. Materialism, on the other hand, has strengthened the bourgeois mind in its capacity to objectify scientific knowledge. Yet even science is separated from the free, conscious activity of the laborer. It is another force of production not subject to conscious control.[61]

Marx maintains that ideas, like other products in bourgeois society, take on a life of their own. While dominant ideas are expressive of the dominant material relationships, Marx argues that the ruling class represents them as universally valid.[62] Marx does not deny the power of ideas in history. He places ideas in a material context. Thus, in capitalism one must distinguish between the reality of material life and the social conception of that reality. For Marx, "Just as one does not judge an individual by what he thinks about himself, so one cannot judge [a social system] by its consciousness."[63]

One interesting illustration provided by Marx is his critique of utility theory. While Marx's comments were directed toward the bourgeois advocates of utilitarianism, they are equally applicable to the neoclassical advocates of subjective utility. Marx objected to the "stupidity of merging all the manifold relationships of people in the *one* relation of usefulness." He argues that this "metaphysical abstraction" derives from modern bourgeois society that conceives of all social relations in monetary and commercial terms. Though there is valid economic content to the utility theory, it is gradually transformed "into a mere apologia for the existing affairs."[64] Inevitably, its presentation as a universally valid theory serves the interests of the capitalist class in its domination of the proletariat.

Marx views each duality he identifies as aspects of a single totality, "distinctions within a unity." Like Hayek, Marx focuses on the mutual interaction of the parts within an "organic whole," which must be understood systemically and historically.[65] In the *Grundrisse*, Marx writes:

> While in the completed bourgeois system every economic relation presupposes every other in its bourgeois economic form, and everything posited is thus also a presupposition, this is the case with every organic system. This organic system itself, as a totality, has its presuppositions, and its development to its totality consists precisely in subordinating all elements of society to itself, or in creating out of it the organs which it still lacks. This is historically how it becomes a totality. The process of becoming this totality forms a moment of its process, of its development.[66]

The *Grundrisse* was not meant for publication, though it was a serious attempt at self-clarification for Marx. And yet, it provides a profound insight into Marx's method. For Marx, the methods of bourgeois science reify the fragmented reality of capitalism. Marx's dialectic attempts to transcend social polarities by identifying them as historically specific to and organically expressive of, the capitalist mode of production. It attempts to transcend the fragmentation within the object of its scrutiny by viewing the system as a totality of dynamic and contradictory processes. The identification of structural contradiction is not problematic for dialectical method. It is fundamental to its framework.

Marx's dialectic is anticipatory, that is, it analyzes polarities in anticipation of their immanent transcendence. It anticipates a historical movement that actualizes the power of conscious human agency, and it reflects this potential for efficacy in the wide-ranging character of its investigatory tools. Marx's dialectic is an integrated methodological response to the division and fragmentation of labor that it confronts in contemporary social science. For Marx, it is a conceptual weapon in the battle against utopian constructivism.

5 Marxian Dialectics

In Chapter One I presented dialectical method as a crucial component of the Hayekian framework. Hayekian dialectics is founded on a doctrine of internal relations that emphasizes the importance of organic unity and context. A thing cannot be abstracted from the historical or systemic conditions that give it meaning. The context is partly constitutive of the thing itself.

In this chapter I examine Marxian dialectics. Though there are important similarities between the Hayekian and Marxian methods, especially with regard to their emphasis on organic unity, Marx focuses on what he calls "contradictory" relationships in social reality. For Marx, these internal contradictions are a dynamic force for social change.

Dialectics versus Determinism

So much has been written on Marx's dialectical method that it is virtually impossible to survey all of the myriad interpretations of its significance. One of the most important debates in Marxist scholarship is whether or not Marx's dialectic is a form of determinism. This view has been expressed by many opponents of Marxism, but it has also been promoted by sympathetic critics, such as Jeffrey Alexander in his comprehensive work on *Theoretical Logic in Sociology*.[1] Alexander offers a well-reasoned case that Marx's thought, especially in the period from 1845 to 1848, laid the foundation for sociological instrumentalism. Marx banishes voluntarism from sociology and "presents an extraordinarily one-sided portrait of social order and the action that informs it."[2] For Alexander, Marx's division between material life and consciousness, or base and superstructure, is ultimately determinist and instrumental, with the base determining superstructural phenomena. Marx, according to Alexander, denies autonomy to the state and to law, and reduces human consciousness to an epiphenomenon of material forces.

Alexander argues that the nondeterminist readings offered by Avineri, Ollman, and Giddens are serious interpretive errors in Marxist scholarship.[3] These interpretations owe much to the methodological revisionism of Frederick Engels. Alexander claims that in the 1890s, Engels's writings introduced an element of indeterminacy into Marx's essentially deterministic theory.

Alexander's viewpoint is to be taken seriously, especially since his book argues against "one-dimensionality" and the "positivist persuasion" in contemporary social science. Alexander wishes "to overcome the dualism of one-dimensional thought" by transcending the dichotomies of fact and value, materialism and idealism, individuality and community.[4] Given the importance of Alexander's stated theoretical intentions, and their dialectical sensibility, his criticism of Marx is particularly compelling.

In a sense Alexander's view is correct, if one focuses on specific periods in Marx's thought that seem to emphasize material and economic factors to the detriment of other factors in social reality. Engels writes, in those celebrated "revisionist" letters of the 1890s:

> Marx and I are ourselves partly to blame for the fact that the younger people sometimes lay more stress on the economic side than is due to it. We had to emphasize the main principle *vis-à-vis* our adversaries, who denied it, and we had not always the time, the place or the opportunity to give their due to the other factors involved in the interaction.[5]

The key word here is "interaction." The dialectic incorporates a thoroughly organic understanding of causality as interaction. Marx and Engels argue that just as economic factors influence noneconomic factors, so too is there a reciprocal influence.

Marx embraces an understanding of internal relations as asymmetric, in which there is an emphasis on material elements. Asymmetric internality is *not* logical dependence. It is *not* a strictly causal relationship. It is an internal relationship in which there is some reciprocity between factors, even though the relation is fundamentally skewed toward one of the factors that is primary.[6] This asymmetry preserves both the hierarchy and internality of the relationship, and prevents vicious circularity. Marx's materialist focus is a theoretical reflection of a historically specific reality. It is, according to Marx, the capitalist mode of production, with its revolutionary material conditions, that seriously affects the mode of his analysis.

The dialectical character of Marx's method is best illustrated by first examining his problematic base-superstructure distinction. It must be understood that Marx's "base" is not purely technological; it is social. It consists of the conscious, material existence of acting human beings. As Marx maintains, the point of departure is "individuals producing in society—hence socially determined individual production."[7] Marx places ontological priority on the "real individuals, their activity and the material conditions under which they live."[8] This is not only the first premise of materialism; it is "the first premise of all human history." People must produce their material means of subsistence. Production is not an abstract category; it is historically specific to particular material conditions and their corresponding social and political relations.

At its core, Marx's understanding of the material base is highly integrated. The base incorporates "activity and mind" which, "in their content and in their *mode of existence*, are social."[9] Human existence is necessarily social, but it is also natural, sensuous, and conscious. These characteristics are inseparable aspects of an organic unity. A person is a living, material object. For Marx, a nonmaterial being is a contradiction in terms, "a creature of abstraction."[10] People live in the material world. They are a part of nature. Human beings are conscious of their own material and sensuous existence, and aware of their own self-consciousness. Their reasoning process is both natural and social. It comprises their nature as human beings, though it develops within existing social conditions.[11] Even language is of a sensuous and social nature because it develops through social interaction and is the very means by which people think.[12]

Marx must deal with the age-old debate between materialists and idealists. His answer contains some ambiguities, but the evidence suggests that he rejected both reductionist materialism and reductionist idealism.[13] "Vulgar" materialists, in Marx's view, identify the world as real and fully material. They see consciousness as a special arrangement of matter. "Vulgar" idealists view material factors as a reflection of states of consciousness. They see existence as partially or wholly constituted by the mind, which gives reality its structure. For vulgar materialists, however, the mind has no reality or nature of its own; it is purely a reflection of brain waves and neural impulses. For vulgar idealists, material reality has no distinctive or objective nature independent of consciousness.

Marx attempts to transcend this materialist-idealist dichotomy. He begins with the primacy of *conscious existence*. First, he rejects the notion that existence has a cause. For Marx, existence exists;

there is nothing prior to, nor posterior to existence. To deny the axiomatic character of this proposition is to forfeit the epistemological validity of one's own denial, since one must exist in order to deny existence as such. For Marx, the belief in "first cause" is then, "a product of abstraction."[14]

Second, Marx views consciousness as an ontological category. Consciousness exists. It is awareness of material existence. It is "directly interwoven with the material activity and the material intercourse of men."[15] It is not an abstraction; it is a faculty of specific, real, living individuals who act "within their given historical conditions and relationships."[16] These conditions shape and are shaped by human activity.

Thus, Marx rejects the vulgar materialist notion of consciousness as a neural reflex. But he equally rejects the idealist notion that abstracts consciousness from its material, historical, and social context. Ideas are not disembodied abstractions. They are generated and absorbed by individuals who live within definite sociohistorical circumstances. Like Hayek, Marx conceives of the human mind as residing within a specific setting. He recognizes that the content of an individual's consciousness is very much a reflection of coexistent conditions. By preserving an internal relationship between existence and consciousness, Marx recognizes the primacy of material factors, even as he projects the possibilities for transformative human agency.

Third, Marx views consciousness not merely as conscious existence, but as conscious, material, *social* existence. The old "perceptual materialism," as Marx calls it, concentrated specifically on the objectivity of the material world, while denying the objectivity of the conscious mind. Marx attempts to transcend this one-dimensionality. His point of departure is a social world that is composed of "sensuous human activity" and the "ensemble of social relationships" that it engenders.[17] The human "species-character" is exemplified in labor, which is life-sustaining, "free, conscious activity."[18]

Labor is not purely instrumental or mechanical. As part of the material base, it is "a process in which both man and Nature participate, and in which man of his own accord starts, regulates, and controls the material re-actions between himself and Nature."[19] For Marx, there is no ultimate duality between nature and society. Individuals are "affirmed in the objective world" as they appropriate nature's substances to human requirements.[20] By acting on the external world, they transform it and actualize their own nature as conscious and social animals.

In a passage from *Capital*, Marx expresses a profound respect for the integrative nature of productive labor, its synthesizing effect on mind and body, its distinctively *human* character:

> A spider conducts operations that resemble those of a weaver, and a bee puts to shame many an architect in the construction of her cells. But what distinguishes the worst architect from the best of bees is this, that the architect raises his structure in imagination before he erects it in reality. At the end of every labour-process, we get a result that already existed in the imagination of the labourer at its commencement. He not only effects a change of form in the material on which he works, but he also realises a purpose of his own that gives the law to his modus operandi, and to which he must subordinate his will. And this subordination is no mere momentary act. Besides the exertion of the bodily organs, the process demands that, during the whole operation, the workman's will be steadily in consonance with his purpose. This means close attention.[21]

Marx conceives of the material base as inclusive of the conscious existence of ontologically real individuals who labor and produce under historically specific conditions. Human existence is both natural and social, and it is characterized by free, conscious activity that is the essence of labor. Labor as such transforms both the external world and the laborer himself. When Marx argues that people's "social existence determines their consciousness," he is providing consciousness with concrete, contextual specificity. Hayek advances this same theoretical position.[22] He argues, however, that while the *contents* of human consciousness are circumscribed in, and relative to, a social and historical setting, the *methods* of consciousness— the means and character of knowledge—are universal and limited. It is true that the human rational faculty has evolved over time. However, no matter how far human knowledge and methods advance, there will always be rules regulating the mind that the "mind in its then prevailing state cannot communicate."[23] This is the self-contradiction of a mind explaining itself, and it is one of the transhistorical invariants in human cognition that blocks the achievement of omniscience. By contrast, Marx suggests that both the contents *and* the methods of awareness are historically conditioned. The problematic implications of this formulation will soon become apparent.

Despite Marx's integrated conception of the material base, both Marx and Engels lend credence to a deterministic interpretation of their works. For instance, though they were not ignorant of the state's involvement in the economy, they often saw political action as irrelevant to economic development. In popularizing their theory, they overstated the importance of purely economic factors in social history. Marx asserts that "the windmill gives you society with the feudal lord; the steam mill, society with the industrial capitalist."[24] This is a particularly one-sided characterization of an otherwise rich dialectical construction.

If grasped as a polemic against Proudhon's *Philosophy of Poverty*, Marx's economistic formulations can be better understood. In the exposition of his theories, Marx always addressed the interests of a specific audience. He often framed his materialist theories in vulgar fashion to combat the equally vulgar idealistic utopian socialists and anarchists with whom he competed.

Engels too, in his reply to Eugen Dühring, overstates the case for economic determinism. He argues that extra-economic factors play *no* part in the evolution of production and exchange. Capitalist monopoly, class society, booms, and crises are caused by purely economic factors, according to Engels. "At no point whatever are robbery, force, the state or political interference of any kind necessary."[25] Engels's claims are both incorrect and ahistorical. Indeed, the developed Marxian perspective parallels Hayek's Austrian view, in its comprehension of the *political* roots of economic crisis.

Marx emphasizes a dialectical relationship between the state and civil society. In Marx's theory, the state serves many contradictory purposes. It provides the illusion of community, even while it serves as the executive committee of the capitalist class. It is a class instrument that also provides for communal needs in class-distorted ways.

Yet Marx views the state—and all extra-economic institutions—as profoundly dependent on material factors, that is, social production. The state is founded on expropriation; "for pillage to be possible, there must be something to be pillaged, hence production."[26] Though Marx recognizes social reality as an intricate, organic totality, his materialist approach acknowledges that production precedes predation—both logically and historically.[27]

Despite this asymmetry between economic and extra-economic factors, Marx opposes strictly deterministic models of social evolution. For instance, in his discussion of the primitive accumulation process, Marx argues "that conquest, enslavement, robbery, murder, briefly force, play the great part."[28] The "disgraceful action of the State" accelerates the accumulation of capital by methods of brute force. The state hastens the capitalist transformation process by crushing outmoded feudal social formations. As Marx writes: "Force is the midwife of every old society pregnant with a new one. It is itself an economic power."[29]

Marx's perspective is not based on historical generalizations. Marx offers an empirical, class analysis. He explains that public debt is "one of the most powerful levers of primitive accumulation." At the dawn of the modern capitalist era, banks, the recipients of political privilege and national titles, advanced money to the state. Aided by a wide network of taxation, the state expropriated the masses. Gradually, self-earned private property was supplanted by capitalistic private property that depended on a form of exploitation immanent to the capitalist production process.[30]

Marx views state involvement in capitalist accumulation as a means of facilitating the inevitable. The state is also a profound source of social and political instability. State involvement in the building of national railways for instance, became a "new source of unbearable state indebtedness and grinding of the masses."[31] In a display of promarket sentiment, Marx suggests on several occasions that a fully free and mobile market with "complete freedom of trade" offers the masses the best possibility for revolutionary transformation in the production process. Based on this transformation, socialism becomes conceivable.[32] In this regard, Marx lamented that Germany, for instance, suffered "from the development of capitalist production [and] from the incompleteness of that development." The survival of "antiquated modes of production" proved to Marx that the German people suffered "not only from the living, but from the dead."[33]

Business Cycle Theory: Marxian-Hayekian Parallels

Though Marx rooted the capitalist class in its ownership of the means of production, class dynamics are not exclusively economic. Marx's description of capitalist crisis transcends vulgar economism. It appreciates fully the crucial role of the state. In many significant ways, it resembles the Hayekian-Austrian theory of the business cycle, though it lacks a sophisticated analysis of relative price discrepancies.[34]

Hayek, like Marx, views the social economy in organic terms. Each aspect of the system is an extension of the other. The market is a dynamic mechanism for the social coordination of production, distribution, and consumption. It transmits knowledge of relative scarcities through the price system. Prices alert entrepreneurs to discrepancies and disequilibria, offering profit opportunities for investment and economic growth.

Hayek and the Austrian economists argue that systemwide discoordination is impossible in a free market. It is an outgrowth of political intervention into the market process. Historically, such discoordination results from an inflationary distortion in the structure of relative prices. It is the necessary by-product of credit expansion through the state-banking nexus.

Inflation dupes the production process into an extension of productive activity due to an artificial lowering of the interest rate. Many investments undertaken during the inflationary boom are *mal*investments since they do not reflect the actual savings-investment ratios. Their liquidation during the depressionary phase of the business cycle is essential. Typically, continued political intervention postpones the reassertion of genuine price patterns. Ultimately the establishment of a central banking system based on fractional-reserve principles facilitates the redistribution and consolidation of wealth and power.

Marx shares with his Austrian rivals an understanding of the *political* character of the business cycle.[35] Yet the implications of his analysis are vastly different. While Hayek argues for the abolition of central banking, and the separation of the political sphere from money and credit,[36] Marx advocates using the credit system as a mechanism for socialist transformation.

Marx believes that capitalism, based on the dualism between purchase and sale, makes an exchange economy necessary. The exchange process makes possible the emergence of pseudotransactions through an inflationary credit system. Like Hayek, Marx views the state as the source of inflation. The state's central bank is the "pivot" of the credit system. Its artificially induced monetary expansion engenders an illusory accumulation process in which "fictitious money-capital" distorts the structure of prices. This leads to overproduction and overspeculation. Real prices—those that reflect actual supply and demand—appear nowhere, until the crisis begins the necessary corrective measures.[37]

Marx views the business cycle as an extension of intensifying class struggle. The state's ability to thrust an arbitrary amount of unbacked paper money into circulation creates an inflationary dynamic that favors debtors at the expense of creditors.[38] The credit system becomes an instrument for the "ever-growing control of industrialists and merchants over the money savings of all classes of society."[39] It provides "swindlers" with the ability to buy up depreciated commodities.[40] Yet the credit system is a historically progressive institution, according to Marx. Despite its distortive effects, it accelerates the expansion of the global market and polarizes classes in capitalist society. It facilitates socialized control of production and capital investment.

This brief digression into business cycle theory illustrates the subtle complexities of Marx's dialectical approach. Marx gives asymmetric priority to the material base, but not at the expense of other crucially important factors. Like Hayek, Marx conceives of social reality in organic terms. He advances a reciprocal, rather than linear, conception of causality, such that every precondition of a process "is at the same time its result, and every one of its results appears simultaneously as its pre-conditions."[41] His theory of the business cycle reflects a genuine grasp of the political roots of economic crisis, even as it emphasizes the economic or material base of political structures and processes.

As Engels explains, the materialist conception of history views the "material mode of existence" as the "primary agent." This is not a determinist formula and does not give those "who use it . . . an excuse for *not* studying history."[42] To view the economic factor as the sole determinant is to transform dialectical materialism into a "meaningless, abstract, absurd" theory. Political, ideological, philosophical, religious, racial, literary, artistic, legal, and other factors all play a part in the human drama. These factors "react upon one another and also upon the economic base," but it is this base of material existence that "in the last instance" must assert its primacy. Material relations—in an organic unity with other factors—are the most decisive because they are essential to social sustenance.[43]

Engels's revisionist letters do not introduce indeterminacy into Marxian theory. In the full context of Marx's dialectical approach, the theory is decidedly nondeterministic. For Marx and Engels, "*all* human relations and functions, however and in whatever form they may appear, influence material production and had a more or less decisive influence on it."[44] Marx objected to using his theory of history as an abstract formula imposed externally on the objects of study. Even when one is approaching the analysis of a society that shares the same economic base as one's own, one must take into account the "innumerable different empirical circumstances, natural environment, racial relations, external historical influences, etc.," which are responsible for "infinite variations and gradations in appearance." For Marx, the study is immanent to its context and must be "ascertained only by analysis of the empirically given circumstances."[45]

Thus, the classic dichotomy in Marxist thought between the material or economic base and the political or ideological superstructure is not a strictly causal model of externally related phenomena. The base and the superstructure are organically interrelated. Their mutual dependence does not rule out the possibility of causal relationships, reciprocal effects, or development through "contradiction."[46]

Dialectical "Contradiction"

In his use of dialectical method, Marx frequently employs an unusual understanding of the concept of contradiction. Certain non-Marxist scholars have condemned this notion as muddled and confused. Popper argues, for instance, that the dialectic discards the Aristotelian law of noncontradiction.[47] This suggests that one of the most important conceptual categories in Marxian dialectics is in direct conflict with the very laws of logic.[48] Unfortunately, however, some Marxists lend credence to Popper's mischaracterization. For instance, George Novack asserts that dialectics "overthrows" and "supercedes" Aristotelian logic.[49] Novack unnecessarily separates two very compatible philosophical positions.

On one level, it must be remembered that Aristotle's law of identity states that something cannot be both A and non-A *at the same time or in the same respect.*[50] In this context, dialectical "contradiction" is not a *logical* construct. Dialectical "contradiction" alters the focus; it views the development of A over time. Its ontological and temporal emphasis does not invalidate logical principles. For Marx, A *does* equal A, but A is conceived as a relational unit. As Ollman explains: "given these are 'A's' relations, this is what 'A' must become and, in the becoming, 'A' may be said to obey the law of its own development."[51] That development takes place within an organic whole in which certain processes are both supportive and destructive of one another.

But on another level, Marx's dialectic absorbs the ontological and relational aspects of the original Aristotelian metaphysic. While it is certainly true, as Kolakowski argues, that Marx was a thoroughly German philosopher,[52] it is also true that he inherits significant elements from classical antiquity.[53] Marcuse suggests that it

was Marx's immediate philosophical forebear, Hegel, who had redis-
covered the dynamic character of Aristotle's ontology, which treats
all being as process and movement.[54] Both Marx and Hegel view this
movement as constituting a unity-in-contradiction, an instability, in
Meikle's words, "between what exists and what is in the process of
coming-to-be."[55] This dynamism is captured by the concept, *Aufhe-
bung*, or "sublation," in which each successive moment of a developmental process both preserves and abolishes, maintains and anni-
hilates its previous movements.[56] In a famous reformulation of these
principles, Hegel writes:

> The bud disappears in the bursting-forth of the blossom, and
> one might say that the former is refuted by the latter; simi-
> larly, when the fruit appears, the blossom is shown up in its
> turn as a false manifestation of the plant, and the fruit now
> emerges as the truth of it instead. These forms are not just dis-
> tinguished from one another, they also supplant one another as
> mutually incompatible. Yet at the same time their fluid nature
> makes them moments of an organic unity in which they not
> only do not conflict, but in which each is as necessary as the
> other; and this mutual necessity alone constitutes the life of the
> whole.[57]

Aristotle's metaphysic embodied this simultaneous focus on
both identity and change, being and becoming. Becoming presupposes being. Change presupposes identity. Likewise, all being is
movement, and all identity entails development. In Marx's works,
this Aristotelian emphasis on developmental and organic unity is
historicized. Change constitutes the real nature of capitalism.[58] The
contradictions within capitalism are both actual and potential. They
are actual since they *exist*. They are part of the system's nature. But
they are also potential, since their existence is basic to capitalism's
development over time. Crises that occur within capitalism are real
manifestations of its internal contradictions propelling the system
toward a transcendent resolution.

The methodological influence of Aristotle on Marx has yet to
be fully assessed. Some of the parallels have been examined vari-
ously by Hook, Marcuse, Bernstein, Gould, Meikle, Copleston, and
McCarthy.[59] A full examination of the impact of Aristotle's thought
on Marx's dialectical method is beyond the scope of the current
study. But Marx fully acknowledged Aristotle as "the greatest
thinker of antiquity," who "was the first to analyze so many forms,

whether of thought, society, nature, and amongst them also the form of value."[60]

Like his Hegelian and Marxian successors, Aristotle aimed to transcend philosophical dualisms. He condemned the idealists and materialists of his day, both the Platonists and the Democritean atomists of ancient Greece. For Aristotle, Plato had committed the fallacy of reification; he had inferred the existence of things from an Ideal abstraction. Aristotle aimed to comprehend the universal through the part, grasping the abstraction through an apprehension of the particular.[61] It was his dedication to the real concrete that enabled Aristotle to bridge the gap between universals and particulars. Thus, Aristotle sought to transcend the polarity between ideas *and* sensible objects, mind *and* body. In contrast to the Platonists, he saw a closer affinity between mind and body, arguing that it was only through the corporeal functions of the body that the mind could exercise its distinctive faculties.[62] But in contrast to the atomists, Aristotle maintained the integrity of the whole qua whole.

Like Aristotle before him, Marx does not isolate an abstracted particular from its context, a part from the whole. For Aristotle, as for Marx, everything is part of a system of related things. Aristotle writes:

> When any one of the parts or structures, be it which it may, is under discussion, it must not be supposed that it is its material composition to which attention is being directed or which is the object of the discussion, but the relation of such part to the total form. Similarly, the true object of architecture is not bricks, mortar, or timber, but the house; and so the principal object of natural philosophy is not the material elements, but their composition, and the totality of the form, independently of which they have no existence. . . . a house does not exist for the sake of bricks and stones, but these materials for the sake of the house, and the same is the case with the materials of other bodies.[63]

In his opposition to reification and his comprehension of systemic relations, Marx inherits a dialectical method that is as much an Aristotelian legacy as it is a Hegelian one. Marx absorbs the Hegelian concept of "contradiction," while never discarding Aristotelian logic, or the Aristotelian ontology upon which this dialectic is built. For Marx, the dialectical concept of "contradiction" is relational, not logical. It views each element of a duality as inseparable from the other, since each is a precondition of the other's existence. Things that appear separate and opposed reciprocally presuppose each other. As Robert Heilbroner explains:

> The *logical* contradiction (or "opposite" or "negation") of a Master is not a Slave, but a "non-Master," which may or may not be a slave. But the *relational* opposite of a Master is indeed a Slave, for it is only by reference to this second "excluded" term that the first is defined.[64]

For Marx, within capitalism, there is a conjunction of polarities that propels the social whole toward some kind of resolution. What distinguishes Marx's understanding of contradiction is not merely the coexistence of opposites, but their unstable movement over time. Marx focuses on both the hostility of opposing spheres, as well as their mutual support. When Marx discusses the distinction between capital and wage-labor, for instance, he sees in each the presupposition of the other. "They condition each other," writes Marx, "each brings the other into existence." They constitute "two sides of one and the same relation."[65]

By examining the dynamic movement and development of the capitalist system, Marx incorporates a temporal element into his conceptual categories. Meikle argues convincingly that this temporal emphasis is yet another outgrowth of Marx's Aristotelianism. Like Aristotle, Marx "makes time ontological as a function of the movement and change of real existents."[66] He sees change as immanent to and constitutive of the essence of real entities. For Marx, the central "entity" that must be scrutinized is capitalism, a structured, dynamic system that is a spontaneous, unintended consequence of the intentional interactions of real human individuals.

The Problem of History

Despite the importance of the temporal dimension in Marx's theory, certain problems arise in the application of his approach to the realm of history. In the Hayekian view, Marx's theory of history, particularly in its future orientation, commits a synoptic fallacy. According to Hayek, this epistemic error is the spool from which Marx weaves a utopian vision of communist society.

Marx's inquiry into the nature of capitalism is as much an investigation of its essential forms as it is of its historical tendencies.

Nothing in dialectics forbids Marx from projecting into the future his understanding of those changes that may be immanent to, and expressive of, the logic of the system. For Marx, communism is a resolution of the internal contradictions of capitalism. In keeping with the Aristotelian tradition, Marx recognized potentiality in actuality.[67] He believed that the potential for socialism emerged from the actual historical and systemic conditions that capitalism provided.

To locate potentiality in actuality is not to embrace a fully teleological view of history. Ollman argues that Marx's approach to the study of history is an outgrowth of his doctrine of internal relations. From the synchronic perspective, Marx studied the system in terms of its multiple interrelationships, such that each factor was both the precondition and result of every other factor. From the diachronic perspective, Marx studied systems in terms of their intertemporal preconditions and results. Just as the present cannot be what it is in the absence of its relationship to the past, so the future cannot be abstracted from the present out of which it will emerge. Ollman explains that Marx studied history "backward." Marx begins with the present and inquires as to its preconditions. Starting with the present, Marx was able to reconstruct history with specific criteria that were relevant to the conditions of the society in which he lived.[68]

While Marx's study of the present helps him to comprehend the past, his speculations on the near, middle, and distant future are extended moments of the present as he understands it. Marx projects the present tendencies within capitalism toward their dynamic resolution over time. Just as the feudal past was the precondition of the capitalist present, so too is the capitalist present the precondition of a communist future.[69]

But Marx's projection of an emergent communist society was highly abstruse. Marx refused to engage in utopian system-building *on principle* because his historical method militated against such constructivism. From the Hayekian standpoint, however, Marx proposed a vision that necessarily depended on privileged access to information on the ultimate goal of human history. While Marx recognizes that societies evolve over time, his distant future speculations suggest a belief in the ultimate triumph of fully efficacious humanity. Thus, the realization of communism is not primarily a political or social achievement; it is essentially epistemological. People would have to attain complete knowledge of social reality, generating precisely determined effects, while transcending unintended social consequences.

To question Marx's historical forecast is not to condemn the future orientation of dialectical method. All social science methods embody assumptions about the future. Both Marx and Hayek embrace a mode of inquiry that unifies content and context. They adopt an immanent view of social change that depends on an assessment of a system's potentials and internal tendencies. But in Hayek's view, future projections must incorporate humility about the possible state of our knowledge of complex, changing societies. To do more than speculate on the possibilities of historical development is to commit what Hayek has termed a "synoptic" fallacy.

For Marx, however, immanent critique anticipated revolutionary change. Uniting theory and practice, Marx declared: "The philosophers have only *interpreted* the world in various ways; the point is to *change* it."[70] Socialism for Marx, offers a profound transformation. It promises the resolution of the dualism between "subjectivism and objectivism, spiritualism and materialism, activity and suffering."[71]

6 The Marxian Utopia

Marx's critique of dualism in capitalist society carries within it the seeds of an historical resolution. Marx views communism as a spontaneous, emergent product of historical development, immanent to the capitalist system itself.

Hayek also views change as immanent to its context. What separates Marx from Hayek, however, is an epistemological assumption about the efficacious potential of reason. Whereas Hayek views the bounds of reason as ontologically or existentially given, Marx sees these limitations as historically conditioned. Eschewing the Hayekian strictures, Marx views the distinction between human intentions and unintended consequences as historically specific to precommunist social formations. He suggests that genuine human history begins with the triumph over this polarity. The communist society, for Marx, will be the product of conscious human agency. Much of the substance of this chapter is devoted to the clash of Marxian and Hayekian theory over these specific epistemological issues.

Socialism As a Product of Spontaneous Order

As an anti-utopian, Marx opposed the creation of blueprints for a socialist future. The very possibilities and forms of change were unpredictable, in Marx's view, because they were immanent to the system from which they emerged spontaneously. Because of his own apprehension regarding the projection of a future communist society, Marx left both his followers and his critics with a difficult task. Invariably, every commentator on the Marxian vision has been compelled to make inferences with regard to the character of postcapitalist society. My discussion here is no exception.

For Marx speculative knowledge of the historical process is useful only as a means of shortening and lessening the birth pangs.[1]

Marx writes that emerging communist society "is in every respect, economically, morally and intellectually stamped with the birth marks of the old society from whose womb it emerges."[2] Communist society would dispense with market exchange. The common ownership of the means of production would multiply the abundance it inherits from its capitalist predecessor, though it would retain certain bourgeois-inspired categories.

Ultimately, socialism would signify "the *development of the richness of human nature as an end in itself.*"[3] For Marx liberation is not an abstract or mental act. It is a historical act "brought about by historical conditions."[4] It could only emerge from a complex, dynamic, spontaneous process of historical development.[5] Since man draws his knowledge from the world around him, it is this world that "must be so arranged that he experiences and gets used to what is truly human in it, that he experiences himself as man." In Marx's view, "If man is formed by circumstances, then circumstances must be made human."[6]

Capitalism is a revolutionary historical achievement but it is, according to Marx, an obstacle to the development of truly human social conditions. The polarities it engenders have profoundly fragmented social life to the point where extraneous objective forces seem to govern the movement of history. If people are to gain a collective capacity to translate their plans into social action with fully determined effects, then it is this historical movement itself that must be directed consciously. The class that must lead this revolution is the proletariat, which becomes the agent of its own transformation.

This revolution does not depend on utopian constructivism, according to Marx. It is historically possible because it is, in the words of Engels, "the necessary consequence of the capitalistic form of production and of the social dualistic antagonism created by it."[7] Capitalism is then, "the last antagonistic form of the social process of production." Human "prehistory" would be brought to an end. As people become the masters of their own fate, their real history would begin.[8]

It must be remembered that this ultimate achievement is itself the product of a two-stage process. According to Marx, the development of capitalism leads to a greater pronouncement in the dualities it generates. These internal contradictions cannot be resolved within the capitalist system. Hence, capitalism will be "burst asunder" in a natural process of immanent systemic collapse. This process would not be as violent or as protracted as the emergence of capitalism from feudalism. Since capitalism develops the social and technolog-ical character of the production process, it provides a strong founda-tion for socialism. The great mass of the proletariat would expropri-ate the property of the minority capitalist class and centralize the means of production in the hands of the state.

Engels asserts that once the state takes possession of the means of production it would be "its last independent act as a state." The state's interference in the social process would become superfluous as "the government of persons is replaced by the administration of things."[9] Under "new, free social conditions," the proletariat will "throw the entire lumber of state on the scrap heap."[10]

In the first stage of communism, the state would be an instru-ment in the hands of workers. It would use coercion to defeat its adversaries and to build a socialized system of production. It would not prohibit an individual's "personal appropriation of the products of labour"; its aim is to end the private ownership of the means of production. Hence, it must engage in what Marx and Engels describe as "despotic inroads in the right of property."[11] *The Communist Manifesto* explains the precise nature of such "despotic inroads." They would include: abolition of landed property and the right of inheritance, the confiscation of rebels' property,[12] a heavy progressive income tax, the centralization and monopolization of credit in the hands of the state, the establishment of a national bank, the cen-tralization of the means of communication and transportation, state ownership of factories and capital, the cultivation of waste lands, the improvement of soil through the planned combination of agri-culture and industry, and country and town, the equal liability of all to labor, the elimination of child labor, and the establishment of industrial and agricultural armies, free education and public schools.[13]

To project the expansion of state power in the service of a socialist politics was, for Marx, a natural extension of the state's instrumental role in capitalism. In Marx's view, capitalists often seek "refuge in forms which, by restricting free competition, seem to make the rule of capital more perfect, but are at the same time the heralds of its dissolution and of the dissolution of the mode of pro-duction resting on it."[14]

Interestingly, both Marx and Hayek view increased state inter-vention as a sign of the dissolution of capitalist economy. Hayek contends that the distortions in contemporary capitalism are ulti-mately traceable to monopolistic elements that were remnants of a precapitalist era. These distortions are consequences of state action:

directly, through interventionist policies; or indirectly, through inappropriate changes in the legal framework of the competitive market order.[15]

By contrast, Marx maintains that state intervention foreshadows the arrival of socialist economy. Marx does not see interventionism as external to the market process. Engels ridicules the Manchester liberals for precisely this characterization. The Manchester bourgeoisie, according to Engels, condemns as socialism every interference by the state into the economy. But Engels believes that such interference is both feudal reaction, and a pretext for exploiting the working class directly.[16] It is not contrary to free competition, but an inevitable consequence of its development.

This immanentist view of the interventionist dynamic is also reflected in the Marxian theory of the state's origins. Marx and Engels argue that the state was founded on certain spontaneously emergent social functions. The safeguarding of common interests and the adjudication of disputes endowed certain men with a measure of authority. As the productive forces increase, these men attain a degree of relative autonomy from the society that they safeguard. Partly through functional heredity, this authoritative group constitutes the state apparatus. The state appears as an illusory community, even as it becomes the organ of class domination, the instrument by which the wealthier classes consolidate their economic and political power.

In the second stage of communism, however, the state would lose its political character and wither away. It would be placed "into the museum of antiquities, by the side of the spinning wheel and the bronze axe."[17] Class distinctions would disappear as the proletariat sweeps away those conditions that generate class antagonism. Gradually, the proletariat would abolish "its own supremacy as a class." Bourgeois inequality would give way to postscarcity and the society would live by the principle: "From each according to his ability, to each according to his needs!" Even the revolutionary dictatorship of the proletariat would become superfluous as the state loses its political character.[18] Society would become a true community, an "association, in which the free development of each is the condition of the free development of all."[19]

The second—and highest—stage of communism would be, for Marx, the ultimate transcendence of dualism. In place of the distinction between appearance and essence, communism would provide an undistorted reality. The form of freedom heralded by the capitalist system in its bourgeois celebration of reason, would be concretized by a content—or social context—which makes free choice both rational and emancipatory. Reason would be actualized by social conditions that are rational. Free, conscious human being would be actualized by social conditions that are free. Body and mind, reason and emotion, knowledge and labor, product and producer would each be united with the other. The alienation of labor's product would be a distant memory. The advanced state of production would lead to an abundance of material and spiritual goods. The dichotomy between mental and physical labor would vanish. Labor would become "life's prime want," both a "free manifestation" and an enjoyment of life itself. Labor would be humanized as each person objectifies their own individuality and sociality. As Marx writes in poetic prose: "in my individual activity I would have immediately *confirmed* and *realized* my true *human* and *social* nature."[20]

In communist society, ideas that were once disconnected abstractions, would create new conditions of life. Engels explains that as people "understand in advance the necessity of changing the social system . . . on account of changing conditions . . . [they] will desire the change before it forces itself upon them without their being conscious of it or desiring it."[21] The producers will have "a perfect understanding" of social forces, which are "transformed from master demons into willing servants."[22] Social organization, the laws of social action, the "extraneous objective forces" of history, "hitherto standing face to face with man as laws of nature foreign to, and dominating him," will

> pass under the control of man himself. Only from that time will man himself, with full consciousness, make his own history—only from that time will the social causes set in movement by him have, in the main and in a constantly growing measure, the results intended by him.[23]

Despite its effuse character, Marx's vision does not pose as a constructivist design. Marx emphasizes that freely associated people would consciously regulate society

> in accordance with a settled plan. This, however, demands for society a certain material ground-work or set of conditions of existence which in their turn are the spontaneous product of a long and painful process of development.[24]

The emphasis here, is on *spontaneous*, evolutionary social order. Like Hayek, Marx views the social process as spontaneous and undesigned. But unlike Hayek, Marx argues that once people have reached the highest stage of communism, the social process is neither spontaneous nor the product of unintended consequences. It is consciously directed by a highly efficacious collective humanity.

For Marx the projected achievement of communist society signals the triumph of human reason. People would no longer be ruled by the blind forces of society or nature. They would achieve a rational regulation of their natural and social existence "with the least expenditure of energy and under conditions most favourable to, and worthy of, human nature."[25] Unintended social consequences would be virtually transcended by the efficacious, highly rational and creative, conscious decisions of collective humanity. According to Engels this does not mean that humanity attains—or can attain—omniscience, nor does it mean that historical development comes to an end.[26] The realm of necessity—that realm which requires continued material production and social reproduction—would remain. But "beyond it begins the development of human energy which is an end in itself," writes Marx, "the true realm of freedom, which, however, can blossom forth only with this realm of necessity as its basis."[27]

The Marxian vision is dependent on an implicit, epistemic transformation that would end the fragmentation and division of labor and knowledge. According to Marx, under capitalism, capital has a monopoly of knowledge and skill. These appear as attributes of capital in the machinery it owns and the forces of production that it commands. These forces "are *organs of the human brain, created by the human hand*; the power of knowledge; objectified."[28] The capitalist, who makes use of the machinery, "need not understand it." As physical and mental labor are divided, so too, do "knowledge and labour become separated."[29] The market flourishes because of this intrinsic fragmentation of knowledge and labor. Marx recognizes that markets perform crucial epistemological functions, such that

> institutions emerge whereby each individual can acquire information about the activity of all others and attempt to adjust his own accordingly. . . . This means that although the total supply and demand are independent of the actions of each individual, everyone attempts to inform himself about them, and this knowledge then reacts back in practice on the total supply and demand.[30]

This incessant movement makes possible the suspension of the ignorance of one's "old standpoint" because of greater access to information.[31] It is for this reason that supply and demand never cease to act. The concept of equilibrium, according to Marx, does not explain anything.[32] It is the market process which, in the "anarchy" of its movement, generates a spontaneous order that is not part of any-one's intentions. In almost Hayekian fashion, Marx shows a keen awareness of the cognitive function of the price mechanism. For Marx, however, socialism would dispense with markets and prices, because it would transcend fragmentation, achieving an epistemic integration that is inherently beyond the reach of the market process.

It is in this sense perhaps, that new insight can be gained from Avineri's observation that epistemology "becomes the vehicle for shaping and moulding reality."[33] Avineri argues that alienation is indicative of a dichotomy between subject and object. Socialist uni-fication would transcend the "distorted process of cognition." By uniting subject and object in the labor process, Marx aims for an undistorted, unfragmented form of social knowledge. In this manner, Althusser too grasps that socialism will make comprehensible even the tacit realm of "skill-production" and "know-how," since the current ways in which people work, their norms, values, and self-conceptions are all ideological reflections of capitalism and its cor-responding class structure.[34] Thus, the Marxian resolution implies the articulation of tacit knowledge in the transition to socialism. As the market process is transcended, epistemic fragmentation would be brought to an end. Socialism would unite knowledge and labor, providing the basis for a revolutionary change in the character of the production process. Through this integration, the collective would achieve a higher level of competence in its application of social plans to material conditions.

Marx's permanent political, social, and economic revolution presumes that such an epistemic achievement is possible. It is on this issue that Marx and Hayek are profoundly opposed.

On the Feasibility of Socialism: Hayek versus Marx

The projected epistemic transformation provokes a classic con-frontation between F. A. Hayek and Karl Marx, between the Austrian school of economics and Marxist theory, between capitalism and socialism. One of the first rounds in this confrontation occurred in the 1920s in an intellectual dialogue that is known today, as the "socialist calculation" debate.[35] Even critics on the left, such as Hilary Wainwright, confirm that Hayek's "exploration of the very character of economic knowledge" lies at the base of the Austrian critique, and that his "new" and "subversive" challenge remains "unanswered" to this day.[36] Since this debate has broad implications for all forms of utopianism, it is useful to discuss some of its aspects here.

The Austrian school arose out of the works of Carl Menger, Friedrich von Wieser, and Eugen von Boehm-Bawerk. The Austrians have made important contributions to subjective value, capital, interest, monetary, banking, and business cycle theory. The early school engaged in explosive intellectual exchanges with the German Historicists on the nature of social science methodology. In the twentieth century, the Austrian tradition was carried on in the works of Mises and Hayek.[37]

Austrians and Marxists have always had a unique ability to raise similar, fundamental questions. Both schools of thought have been intellectually influenced by the constellation of Aristotelian, German, and Scottish traditions.[38] Both share the view that social reality is a dynamic process constituted by human action. Both criticize mainstream, static, equilibrium-based economic analysis. Both refuse to separate the economic sphere from the organic social whole of which it is a part.[39] Their vibrant and colorful intellectual relationship began in the late nineteenth century, in the historic debate over Marx's theory on the transformation of value into price.[40] It has continued to the present day.

The calculation debate is about the ability of a socialist society to plan economic growth in the absence of market prices. Mises, Hayek's Austrian mentor, accepted Marx's identification of socialism with the transcendence of the market and capitalist social relations. In an original 1920 essay on "Economic Calculation in the Socialist Commonwealth," Mises argues that without a market and its pricing mechanism, there is no means by which to calculate the production of capital goods on which all future consumption is based.[41] Entrepreneurs in the capital goods sector rely on monetary means in their rational calculation of investment decisions. Prices provide the entrepreneur with information on relative scarcities. Any proposed process of establishing shadow prices, as advocated by market socialists,[42] could not possibly duplicate the subtle, sophisticated complexity of the price mechanism in its dynamic ability to transmit relevant data to entrepreneurial decision-makers.

Hayek's evolutionist perspective has had a profound impact on the calculation debate. Hayek contends that knowledge dispersed among social actors cannot be known to any one mind, or controlled by any centralized agency. The extended order sustains—and is sustained by—a competitive procedure of discovery.[43] Hayek writes:

> The market is the only known method of providing information enabling individuals to judge comparative advantages of different uses of resources of which they have immediate knowledge and through whose use, whether they so intend or not, they serve the needs of distant unknown individuals. This dispersed knowledge is *essentially* dispersed, and cannot possibly be gathered together and conveyed to an authority charged with the task of deliberately creating order.[44]

Hayek demonstrates the comprehensive nature of his approach. From the vantage point of epistemology, Hayek denies that people can gain a synoptic grasp of the social totality. Human action generates unintended social consequences that coalesce, forming an extended spontaneous order that is no part of anyone's conscious design. Hayek expresses these same insights from the vantage point of political economy. For Hayek no individual can plan social order transcendentally. The rivalrous competition of the market process generates price information. Without such a market process, the data are not generated. Thus, "the extended order *circumvents* individual ignorance" and links each individual "in chains of transmission through which he receives signals enabling him to adapt his plans to circumstances he does not know."[45] The complexity of markets is generated by the reciprocal alignment and realignment of individuals with one another.[46] Lavoie reiterates this Hayekian insight:

> If knowledge is dependent upon the process or context from which it springs, then any partial interference with either of them may, if significant and persistent enough, threaten to subvert the knowledge itself.[47]

Thus, the Austro-Hayekian argument is an epistemic justification of the market. The cognitive function of the price mechanism is internal to the operation of the market itself, and once severed from its context, the intricate, complex data lose their concrete significance. The data have significance because they emerge from the social interactions of market participants, with their own plans, and interpretive frameworks. For Hayek, the state's persistent intervention in the market process can only subvert the generation of knowledge on which the extended order is based.

The Austrian argument utilizes the Hayekian-Polanyian distinction discussed in Chapter Three, which views knowledge as sometimes tacit, sometimes articulate. Knowledge is both qualitative and quantitative, integrated rather than merely cumulative. The market is a means of synthesizing the knowledge of acting individuals, multiplying the power of their cooperative collaboration beyond the sum of their individual efforts.[48] Paradoxically, as the market provides the context for the articulation of individual goals, it enables people to economize on the need for explicit articulation. A complex, technological society advances by means of a price system that continuously condenses vast amounts of integrated information.

The market is a learning process. "Learning," observes Lavoie, "is an enhancement of our interpretive powers and of our tacit understanding of unfolding reality rather than the simple accumulation of data."[49] Entrepreneurial decision-making relies not merely on the raw quantifiable data of prices, but on the entrepreneur's know-how, which is embedded in the habitual productive activity, the skills and specialties of rivalrous market competitors. The essence of entrepreneurial creativity is this tacit, qualitative dimension of knowledge.[50] It is through market production and exchange that a "social" intelligence emerges that is greater than the intelligence of each individual market participant.[51] This is the market's distinctive mechanism for promoting efficacious action among its individual participants. People will never be the complete masters of their destiny. But the market enables partially knowing individuals to better apprehend and command nature, not merely in an instrumental manner, but as competent, purposeful, and creative human actors in a spontaneous social setting.

Hence, though both Marx and Hayek recognize the fragmentation of knowledge, it is Hayek who believes that knowledge is *essentially* dispersed. Even as Hayek grasps the organic unity of the spontaneous order, he continues to reject strict organicity and the synoptic delusion on which it rests. He views the market as the best means of coordinating fragmented information. His epistemological defense of the market is one that has broad political implications as well.

Hayek asserts that socialists despise capitalism because their constructivist rationalist principles rebel against the evolutionary morals and institutions that the capitalist system requires. He argues that socialism is "based on demonstrably false premises" that endanger "the standard of living and the life itself of a large proportion of our existing population."[52] His defense of the market translates into a compelling critique of state planning, one which has particular significance since the fall of the Communist bloc.

The historical experience of the former Soviet Union is a testament to the difficulty of planning without a price mechanism. Soviet central planners were unable to suppress those subtle market forces on which their future economic growth depended. The Soviet system owed its survival to a de facto market process of bribery, corruption, under-the-counter sales, hoarding, and black-market entrepreneurship. The Soviet entrepreneur or *tolkach* linked state-run factories to the black market, and discovered scarce resources to supplement systemic shortfalls.

Nevertheless, the Soviet's static and arbitrary price policy became a chief obstacle to technological innovation and social mobility. Such thinkers on the left as Robert Heilbroner have written of the "great tragedy" of the Soviet system. Central planning could not achieve economic coordination; it generated grotesque misallocations, inefficiencies, and bureaucratization. In an oft-cited comment, Heilbroner declares: "It turns out, of course, that Mises was right." Under socialism, "as Mises foresaw, setting prices became a hopeless problem, because the economy never stood still long enough for anyone to decide anything correctly."[53]

Back in 1944, Hayek admonished the "socialists of all parties" to abandon central planning. He argued that socialism undermined the rule of law by legitimating the social relationships of authority and coercion.[54] Inevitably, the "internal contradictions" of state planning threatened the fabric of the civilized, extended order, while destroying the subtle, yet powerful, market forces on which prosperity was built.[55] For many observers on both the left and the right, the twentieth-century collapse of Communism is a vindication of the Misesian-Hayekian critique.

Wainwright has suggested however, that Hayek's opposition to centralized social engineering is primarily derived from his "individualistic" assumptions about the character of knowledge, his belief that social change cannot be consciously and collectively directed. The problem with central planning, in Wainwright's view,

> is not that it aims at conscious social change. Rather it presumes that the most effective operators of social change, whether a social democratic state or a Leninist party, are acting on society from the outside—just as on a positivistic model the social scientist analyses from outside, without any self-consciousness of the social relations and processes connecting them and the subject of their study.[56]

But this is precisely the point of Hayek's more general, dialectical approach. Hayek objects to the illusory notion that people can rise above their society to judge and control it "from the outside or from a higher point of view . . ." Social change must always be based on "the material that is available, and which itself is the integrated product of a process of evolution."[57] Even as Hayek recognizes the organic unity of an evolving, spontaneous order, he rejects the utopian belief that it is possible to attain a synoptic view of that order. Since partially knowing human actors are among the internal, constituent elements of the social whole, they can only achieve a particularized vantage point within the totality. As social actors in possession of both articulated and tacit knowledge, people may "tinker with parts of a given whole" but never "entirely redesign it."[58]

Complete, externally directed societal reconstruction is the stated aim of the central planners in Hayek's view. But modern technocratic elites have been unable to control each and every aspect of social reality. Their inevitable "totalitarianism" is an outgrowth of their futile attempts to actualize an ideal as if they possessed total knowledge. Their one-dimensional, constructivist resolution of the statist dualism between state and civil society, leaves nothing but brutality and oppression in its wake.[59]

As a critique of state planning, Hayek's argument is persuasive. But as a critique of Marx's theory of social transformation, the Hayekian argument raises important questions about the feasibility of communism in particular, and the dangers of utopian theorizing in general. Of course Marx's vision of communism is vastly different from the path that Hayek warned against. Marx would have probably dismissed contemporary Communism as historically premature. Yet the Hayekian perspective is as opposed to Marx's historical vision as it is to any "premature" manifestations.

Marx's project presumes that the victorious proletariat would not be hampered by the material constraints encountered by modern-day central planners. Nevertheless, the worker's state would have a grandiose task before it: the market would be replaced by a command economy; private ownership of the means of production would cease; the price system would be operative no longer; and the state would monopolize credit, communication, transportation, and other key economic sectors. In the first transitional stage to communism, people would not yet have the ability to implement their plans without generating substantial unintended social consequences. This is a state of affairs that Marx foresees only in the second—and highest—stage.

Marx argues that capitalism itself would bring about the disso-lution of its own spontaneous order. But Marx faces a theoretical paradox. The market price system, he says, loses its effectiveness because of deepening capitalist crises. The first stage of communist society would dispense with the price mechanism altogether even though it is a long way from the realization of full collective control. Hence, its use of the state to embark on a measured course toward full communism must engender significant unintended social con-sequences. As both Hayek and Popper maintain, the social world does not stop functioning in the process of its reconstruction. Lack-ing the tools of a fully efficacious planning process, the proletarian state would be unable to achieve all that it sets out to do.

Marx acknowledges that the proletarian state can generate cer-tain isolated "counter-revolutionary" consequences. But he sees these abuses by specific state officials as marginal and transitional. Certain revolutionists, "men of a different stamp," could hamper the development toward communism. Though these men were "an unavoidable evil," Marx suggests that "with time they are shaken off," whether through democratic election or recall.[60]

But Marx does not grasp the structural dimensions or com-plexities of the problem. For Hayek unintended social consequences are not traceable solely to specific abusers of power. Without a fully efficacious planning mechanism, socialist planners generate unin-tended consequences *by necessity*. These consequences are internal to the structural dynamic of the society as a whole, and hence, far more insidious. Moreover, since people cannot achieve such absolute control over human destiny, the proletariat would remain a captive of those very state institutions that it is unable to transcend. The withering away of the state would be postponed indefinitely.

In Hayek's view no individual or group of individuals is capable of consciously producing desired effects on a social scale, while blocking the emergence of unintended consequences. To accom-plish this feat, people would have to know and articulate the precise effects of each of their actions. Even the tacit component of human knowledge could not escape the necessity for articulation.

By contrast, the extended order of the market takes advantage of inarticulate knowledge in a way which does not demand its explicit articulation. According to Hayek a price, within the con-text of the vast system that generates it, transmits knowledge to entrepreneurs who are themselves participants in a dynamic com-petitive rivalry. The success of Marx's communism would require a thoroughly new epistemic context, one that somehow transcends the *essential* dispersion of human knowledge among partially knowing social actors.

Marx suggested, however, that the fragmentation of knowledge is perpetuated by the market itself. He argued that the market depends on the continued survival of dualistic distinctions, including the polarities between knowledge and labor, appearance and essence, form and content, and intentions and unintended consequences. To have doubts about humanity's capacity to bridge these distinctions is to exhibit one's historically specific ignorance. The very fragmentation within capitalist society makes a vision of unification inconceivable. Communism, for Marx, makes the implausible seem possible.

Ultimately, what separates Marx from Hayek is an epistemological assumption about the efficacious potential of the human mind. Hayek rejects Marx's historical projections for their reliance on constructivist and synoptic fallacies. Despite his own opposition to utopianism, Marx, in Hayek's view, proposed a resolution that remained on the precipice of utopia. For Hayek, *"Man is not and never will be the master of his fate."*[61] He writes:

> Freedom means that in some measure we entrust our fate to forces which we do not control; and this seems intolerable to those constructivists who believe that man can master his fate—as if civilization and reason itself were of his making.[62]

Marx's communism would require, in Hayek's estimation, that "every action would have to be judged as a means of bringing about known effects."[63] This presumes that people are capable of omniscience, something that is not possible to them.[64] The achievement of Marx's historical projections would require a different kind of species: not a partially knowing human being, but an entity capable of total knowledge. By seeing human action as productive of effects that can be known in advance, Marx projects a future epistemic achievement that has never been realized in any previous historical epoch.

For contemporary societies, however, the choice is not between total ignorance and total knowledge. Critics on the left presume that transformed social relations might provide people with an enhanced ability to achieve certain desired effects in their activities.[65] Invariably, however, such proposals for the establishment of nonmarket, "nonauthoritarian," "autonomous" agencies of social change rely on the state for their legitimacy. This is a far cry from the Marxian vision. Engels writes, for instance, that "so long as the proletariat still *uses* the state, it does not use it in the interests of freedom . . . and as soon as it becomes possible to speak of freedom, the state ceases to exist. We would therefore propose to replace *state* everywhere by . . . community."[66]

For Marx and Engels the use of political mechanisms might provide workers with a greater sense of control over their own lives. But this is not the goal of—nor is it a substitute for—Marx's vision of communism. If workers are unable to get beyond their sustained use of the coercive state, if they are unable to get beyond those unintended—and perhaps, undesirable—consequences of state action, then Marx's vision can degenerate into a reactionary, authoritarian nightmare.

Why would a thinker of Marx's stature and analytical abilities propose such a problematic historical forecast? Hayek suggests that, despite his anti-utopianism, Marx remained a captive of the Enlightenment and its constructivist-rationalist notions of Reason, "with a capital *R*."[67] Unlike the rationalists, however, Marx was prone to historicize *everything*, including the nature of his own theories. On these grounds Marxists might reject Hayekian strictures as a pure reification of contemporary epistemic conditions. They might contend that Hayek suffers from a synoptic delusion of his own, since he assumes that there is a transhistorical limit to human cognitive potential. Indeed, it seems as if Hayek has projected epistemic strictures as if *he* had knowledge of the ultimate *limits* of human knowledge.

Marxist philosophers, such as Marx Wartofsky, have argued that "it remains an empirical question whether there are transhistorical invariants in the history of cognition."[68] If this is indeed an empirical issue, then it may only be resolved by some very distant, future generation. But if the Hayekian strictures are *existential*, rather than historical, then the Marxian project, in all its variants, has embraced an inherently utopian, unreachable goal.

Sensing the importance of these issues, Critical thinkers have taken up the Hayekian challenge. Their response is the subject of the next chapter.

7   The Challenge of a New Left

In his vision of the ideal communist society, Marx projects profound epistemic changes with implications both social and individual. Communist man and woman would be individual embodiments of a superior collective. Invoking Nietzschean imagery in a now familiar passage, Trotsky reminds us that in the future society proposed by Marx,

> Man will . . . raise himself to a new plane, to create a higher social biologic type, or, if you please, a superman. It is difficult to predict the extent of self-government which the man of the future may reach or the heights to which he may carry his technique. Social construction and psycho-physical self-education will become two aspects of one and the same process. . . . Man will become immeasurably stronger, wiser and subtler; his body will become more harmonized, his movements more rhythmic, his voice more musical. The forms of life will become dynamically dramatic. The average human type will rise to the heights of an Aristotle, a Goethe, or a Marx. And above this ridge new peaks will rise.[1]

Thus, communism would necessarily entail a grand psychosocial transformation. In the new society, individuals would exhibit a degree of competence that would transcend the technical mastery of production skills. These very skills would be fully articulated as a means to the conscious control of social production. And as the society would gain control over its collective destiny, the individual would gain control over his own cognitive functions, their evaluative and emotional content, and the very processes that give rise to them. In Trotsky's formulation, as in Marx's, there is the implicit assumption that people *can* and *will* become the masters of their own destiny, grasping both articulated and tacit dimensions of mind.

Indeed, Hilary Wainwright has observed that Marx fully understood "the tacit and particular insights of experience," but "he never translated such general notions into principles of political agency." Ultimately, Marx saw political parties and institutions as practical instruments for the achievement of socialist goals. For Wainwright, as for Hayek, this instrumentalism became the basis of rigid, Leninist and Stalinist models for state-guided revolution.[2]

Wainwright, Habermas, and other theorists on the left have fleshed out the full epistemic implications of the Marxian vision. These thinkers have embraced ideals of "radical" or "participatory" democracy that are less state-centered.[3] Their contributions are important since they directly challenge the Hayekian perspective. Hence, a brief examination of their "arguments for a new left" provides a useful postscript to our study.

Habermas and the Reconstruction of Marxism

In the late nineteenth and early twentieth centuries, Marxism began to develop in many different theoretical directions. Perhaps the most provocative intellectual amalgam has emerged out of the Frankfurt School, those Critical thinkers such as Theodor Adorno, Erich Fromm, Max Horkheimer, and Herbert Marcuse who conducted their initial studies at the Institute for Social Research in Germany.[4] Today, Jürgen Habermas remains the most important Critical theorist of his generation.

The Frankfurt school tradition attempted a reconstruction of the Marxian dialectic taking seriously the contributions of non-Marxists, such as Max Weber. Weber objected to Marxism because he interpreted it as a monocausal theory of economic determinism. He identified capitalism as the very embodiment of rationality. Capitalism functioned with instrumental efficiency, precision, and superior economic calculation. But Weber believed that its rationality was purely technical. "Substantive rationality," by contrast, applies to the ends of human action, and not merely the means. Modern corporate and bureaucratic institutions failed to recognize this important normative dimension of action.

The Critical theorists adopted the Weberian distinction between instrumental and substantive rationality. They argued that capitalism created a duality between means and ends. In conjunction with Marx, they claimed that the bourgeoisie fought its greatest battles under the banner of reason but that capitalism itself deprived "reason of its realization,"[5] that is, it stunted the development of institutions that were subject to rational control.

Like Hayek, Habermas argues that it was the rationalistic Enlightenment that had projected an ideal *"utopia of reason."* But like Marx, Habermas argues that the Enlightenment faith was contradicted by the realities of bourgeois life. Still, it was bourgeois capitalism that had enabled specific social classes to reap disproportionately the benefits of a scientific and technological civilization. Only the emergent, fully rational, objective structures of bourgeois society could provide the foundation for a future order in which these structures would be universalized.[6]

In the absence of such universalization, modern technocrats extended the domination of bourgeois science by attempting to design social policy as if they could manipulate the relevant factors and produce the desired conditions for a genuinely human social existence. The practical tasks of politics were replaced by purely technical considerations. Social control through the technical-administrative mechanisms of the state became the primary concern of modern politics.[7]

Like Hayek, the Critical theorists claimed that they were reacting against the scientistic, positivistic, and mechanistic conception of reason that divorced facts from values. They opposed centralization, coercive control of communication, and the bureaucratic regimentation of economic and social relations that were typical of twentieth-century fascist and communist regimes. Science, in the hands of a technocratic elite, had become an ideological tool of social manipulation.[8]

The Frankfurt school attempted to recapture the dialectical method of Marx, while maintaining a Marxist faith in the human triumph over unintended social consequences. Adorno argues that the dialectic offers an immanentist view of social reality. It reflects critically on the context within which it moves. "Its objective goal," Adorno claims, "is to break out of the context from within."[9] This necessitates criticism of the context itself as a means of transcending its stifling limitations.[10]

It is of course, a major question if human beings can *ever* break out of the context within which they live. This is not to deny the reality of social change. But such change can only proceed with a critical knowledge of the distinction between those conditions that are historically specific and those that are universal. For Hayek, radical social theorists must recognize that reason is thoroughly embedded in its social context. No theorist can ever fully rise above this context in an act of total self-transcendence. In contrast to the synoptic implications of Adorno's immanentist critique, Hayek's own approach to immanent criticism allows for a tinkering with the rules of just social conduct even as it remains tied to the traditions it seeks to alter. One can legitimately question whether or not Hayek has provided enough scope for the role of reason, but one cannot disregard his very real insights into the existential limitations of human agency.

Ultimately, however, social existence does not offer us a choice between intended human action and unintended social consequences. It is indeed a question of degree. Though Hayek at times suggests an unrealistic choice between "spontaneous" and "designed" order, his perspective beckons us to explore more fully the *degree* to which people think and act—both consciously and tacitly—so as to fulfill their own long-term survival needs. By emphasizing the existential limits of reason, and the interaction between articulated and unarticulated epistemic and social practices, Hayek's insights can help to define a more realistic context for the radical project.

Critical theorists of a "new left" have begun to deal with these issues.[11] Absorbing significant aspects of the Marxian legacy, these thinkers recognize the very real difficulties in bridging the gap between theory and practice. Some, like Wainwright, have explicitly confronted the Hayekian strictures. Before Wainwright, however, it was Habermas who focused most extensively on the epistemic dimension. Habermas is less interested in criticizing the established order, and more concerned with building a positive alternative to the status quo. Employing tools from phenomenology, psychoanalysis, and hermeneutics, Habermas engages in a self-conscious reconstruction of historical materialism.[12]

This section cannot possibly discuss the full range of Habermas's influential works, especially since his own thought has undergone various incarnations. But Habermas's Critical thought has been recognized by Wainwright as "the stimulating force" behind a variety of social movements that have aimed for a transformative theory and politics of knowledge.[13] A brief examination of Habermas's thought can help us to better understand Wainwright's newest challenge to the Hayekian critique; her own proposals are fully informed by Habermasian themes.

By articulating the broad epistemic requirements of Marx's resolution, Habermas aims to reconstitute historical materialism in altered form so as to make its actualization more plausible. He sees his own contribution as a reaffirmation of the critical self-reflectiveness inherent in the original Marxian formulation. Habermas suggests that historical materialism has been rigidified into a teleological theory. But at its core, Marx's project was *not* teleological; rather, it was oriented toward social praxis. Marx wished to identify the empirical conditions upon which people could engage in practical, transformative social action. For Habermas, Marx's historical resolution was not based on metaphysical necessity, but on the knowledge of objective conditions. If the theory seemed to embody "exaggerated epistemic claims," this was only because its interpreters had ignored "the essentially practical nature of its prospective dimension." Projections of a glorious future were not an exercise in utopian contemplation or scientific prediction. They were anticipations of a practical reason anchored in the real world.[14]

Though Habermas seeks to reconstruct the Marxian resolution, he recognizes that the theory of historical materialism as such, embraced a quasi-synoptic vantage point. Its explanation of social evolution is "so comprehensive that it embraces the interrelationships of the theory's own origins and application." The Marxian theory articulates the conditions under which human beings can reflect objectively on their history. But the theory also addresses a specific class, the proletariat, in whose enlightening self-reflections lies an emancipatory role.[15] It is the nature of this emancipation that is of central concern to Habermasian thought.

Habermas begins his inquiry by drawing from the hermeneutical contributions of Hans-Georg Gadamer. Gadamer emphasized that no theorist could approach social reality as if it were a clean slate. The theorist brings with him a certain constellation or "horizon" of expectations, norms, and practices. This horizon conditions how a theorist views his subject matter. The theorist must grasp the context within which other horizons operate and function. He achieves a "fusion of horizons" by bringing his own conception into dialectical interplay with another point of view. What emerges is an approach to social reality that appropriates the lessons of alternative frameworks through a comprehension of their distinctive way of looking at the world. The interpretive process is then, an exercise in translation.

Extending Gadamer's analysis, Habermas argues that competent communication must be free of distortion, deceit, and manipulation. Habermas's ideal society is one based on nonexploitative social relationships. His reconstruction of the Marxian project constitutes an exploration of its profound epistemic implications. Communism, for Habermas, is a politics that is ultimately dependent on the complete mastery of symbolic interaction.

For Habermas, no social class could achieve emancipation without overturning the structures and relations of power embedded in every aspect of the social system. Habermas views all social systems "as networks of communicative actions."[16] Communicative actions are dialogical interactions between and among social participants who observe norms that are intersubjectively valid.[17] Genuine communicative action is always "oriented to mutual understanding."[18] But the institutions of power depend on and perpetuate a distorted form of social communication. The collective's conscious control of social-production relations can only emerge under political conditions that are free from such distortion.[19]

All social systems anticipate the ideal speech situation, one in which people have mastered the practical art of communication. In order to understand the nature of communicative distortion and hence, social domination, one must first grasp the essence of genuine communication. Distortion is a negativity. Every attempt to distort or deceive relies implicitly on ideal communicative conditions. Even "intentional deception" is ultimately oriented toward truth, since it is truth that it seeks to usurp. In this sense, distorted social dialogue is parasitical and fully dependent on the logic of ideal speech.[20]

For Habermas, in every act of speech there is the implication of an ideal speech situation. In mastering such ideal speech, people move toward the goals of truth, freedom, and justice within the realm of social consciousness, even though these ideals have yet to be actualized in social reality.[21] The intersubjective validity foundations of speech are characterized by Habermas as "universal pragmatics."[22] Habermas argues that in any genuine communication,

> The speaker must choose a comprehensible [*verstandlich*] expression so that speaker and hearer can understand one another. The speaker must have the intention of communicating a true [*wahr*] proposition (or a propositional content, the existential presuppositions of which are satisfied) so that the hearer can share the knowledge of the speaker. The speaker must want to express his intentions truthfully [*wahrhaftig*] so that the hearer can believe the utterance of the speaker (can trust him). Finally, the speaker must choose an utterance that is right [*richtig*] so that the hearer can accept the utterance and speaker and hearer can agree with one another in the utterance with respect to a recognized normative background. Moreover,

communicative action can continue undisturbed only as long as participants suppose that the validity claims they reciprocally raise are justified.[23]

This formulation suggests a mutuality of knowledge, trust, and values. Dialogical partners achieve communicative competence by fulfilling the truth conditions or existential presuppositions of knowledge. In expressing their intentions linguistically, the dialogical partners learn to trust one another. And in conforming to recognized norms of communicative action, the dialogical partners share value orientations.[24]

An "intersubjective mutuality of reciprocal understanding" is the essence of an ideal speech situation. Such a condition is universalized in Habermas's vision of a "dialogical community." The emergence of social understanding is a process in which the participants satisfy the presuppositions of communication and move from the incomprehensible to a full social consensus, a community based on shared knowledge, trust, and values.

This laudable goal requires much more than the ability of human beings to talk to one another. Habermas explains that genuine communication requires the explicit articulation of rules of grammar and idiom. A truly competent speaker must master these rules in order to form comprehensible sentences and communicate them adequately. The speaker will inevitably gain the ability to exert an "illocutionary influence" on his dialogical partner, and vice versa, because every speech act will be anchored in validity claims that are "cognitively testable."[25]

Habermas argues that the explicit articulation of grammatical rules cannot be achieved without the corresponding transformation of "a practically mastered pretheoretical knowledge (know-how) . . . into an objective and explicit knowledge (know-that)."[26] This is the distinction between the tacit and the articulate recognized by such thinkers as Dewey, Ryle, Polanyi, and Hayek. The tacit dimension is embodied in human skills, forming the core of an inarticulate component of mind. People interact by making statements that employ certain tacitly accepted linguistic operations and rules. For Habermas "rational reconstruction" is the basis of transformation because it aims to make explicit these tacit epistemic and practical components. By articulating the contents and the methods of knowledge, dialogical partners can consciously generate intended consequences in their interpersonal relations. Differences of opinion in a rational community will be resolved not through the use of force or fraud, but through a symmetrical and reciprocal dialogue.

A multitude of issues are entailed in this Habermasian formulation. On one level, it can be argued that Habermas's position differs little from Polanyi's basic insights on the nature of true communication. Polanyi writes:

> Spoken communication is the successful application by two persons of the linguistic knowledge and skill acquired by such apprenticeship, one person wishing to transmit, the other to receive, information. Relying on what each has learnt, the speaker confidently interprets them, while they mutually rely on each other's correct use and understanding of these words. A true communication will take place if, and only if, these combined assumptions of authority and trust are in fact justified.[27]

Though this passage suggests a coincidence of views between Polanyian and Habermasian conceptions of rational dialogue, there is in fact, a crucial difference between them. Habermas assumes that the ideal speech situation will make explicit both linguistic knowledge and skill. The tacit component of knowledge would be fully articulated. By contrast, Polanyi, like Hayek, insists that as our definitions become more explicit, and as we articulate rules, we shift the "tacit coefficient of meaning" but "cannot entirely eliminate it."[28] Habermas's ideal speech situation suggests that such a coefficient can be eliminated, leading to the victory of human intentionality and the elimination of unintended social consequences.

The achievement of such an ideal speech situation would require a quasi-libertarian commitment to fully voluntary human relations. Habermas argues that the use of force must be prohibited in the dialogical community. It is not possible for social consensus to be reached through the imposition of agreement by one side on another. Habermas decries domination as a "strategic" form of interaction in which at least one of the participants deceives the other by lying, misleading, or manipulating. A condition of *"systematically distorted communication"* results when the participants are engaged not only in interpersonal deception, but in self-deception as well. Such self-deception involves, at least partially, the obscuring of one's own strategic behavior from oneself.[29]

It is at this stage in his reconstruction that Habermas begins to combine elements of an analytic method with "depth hermeneutics." Depth hermeneutics is psychoanalytic self-reflection that liberates the individual from "unrecognized dependencies." Habermas draws an explicit parallel between Freudian psychoanalytic theory and therapy, and Marxian theory and praxis.[30]

Psychoanalysis is a radical science because it seeks to get to the root of internal corruptions. It seeks to comprehend the "mutilations" that have been internalized by the individual agent. These "mutilations" have meaning as such, and their meanings must be explored if they are to be transcended. Habermas considers the corruptions to be akin to hermeneutical texts. Synthesizing linguistic analysis and psychoanalysis, Habermas argues that depth hermeneutics can make explicit the tacit, causal connections that take place in the individual's subconscious.[31] Psychoanalysis enables the therapist to understand the terms in which the agent deceives himself. The self-deceptions of the agent occur through a series of omissions and distortions, some of which are involuntary and accidental, some of which are intentional. But when these cognitive errors become pervasive they are symptomatic of pathology and cannot be ignored.[32]

Dream interpretation is one of the means by which the therapist can grasp the root of such pathologies. Dreams are texts that confront the author as "alienated and incomprehensible." The analyst must penetrate behind the miasma of distortion in order to grasp its meaning. Not only must the purpose of the distortion be grasped, but the distortion itself—and its role in the agent's life—must be fully comprehended if it is to be transcended. Dream interpretation compels the agent toward a process of self-reflection. The analyst uses spontaneous free association techniques to guide the agent toward the articulation of the dream text.[33]

Habermas recognizes that the agent often resists this articulation process. Such resistance is an obstacle to "free and public communication of repressed contents." Once achieved, however, articulated self-reflection proceeds on a cognitive level even as it "dissolves resistances on the affective level."[34] The analyst must function like a historian or an archaeologist. Reconstructing the agent's early life history, the analyst shifts the tacit coefficient of meaning toward explicit comprehensibility, enabling the patient to derepress those events that have been forgotten, and that are relevant to his current condition. The patient's recollection is the means of his or her own restoration.[35]

What emerges is a reintegration, "the critical overcoming of blocks to consciousness," which "reverses the process of splitting-off." Habermas invokes Hegelian imagery: the ego of the patient recognizes its own alienated self-identity in the now-objectified illness.[36] While the analyst reconstructs that which has been repressed, the patient begins to reappropriate a lost portion of the self.

Habermas's reconstruction concretizes characteristics that were merely implicit in the Marxist ideal. Habermas has put psycho-epistemological flesh on a skeletal Communist superbeing. Such a superbeing would emerge from a lengthy process of psychoanalysis, fully articulating every thought, every emotion, and every action—to him or herself and to each of his or her dialogical partners. But if the radical project must depend on such a profound achievement, then it is difficult to imagine by what means it can be realized—or universalized. As a complement to the Marxian vision, Habermas's proposals, in Hayek's view, embody the same problematic desire for total knowledge.

Habermas's reconstruction, like Marx's, attempts to burst out from its context. And like Marx, Habermas seems to embrace a vision of a rational human society that is synoptic in its implications. While his writings reflect a more thorough grasp of the tacit-articulate distinction than those of his predecessor, he makes the unlikely assumption that people can shift the tacit coefficient of meaning toward virtually complete articulation. Even in his later writings, in his recognition that knowledge acquisition and dissemination occurs through "decentration" of scholarly endeavors, Habermas posits a dialogical community in which this knowledge is fully articulatable.[37] And in more recent published comments, Habermas, though critical of state socialism, continues to endorse the neo-Marxist political ideal of "radical democracy," in which "welfare state measures" are employed "to tame capitalism to some point where it becomes unrecognizable as such."[38]

Hayek did not comment extensively on the Habermasian reconstruction. But he rejected Habermas's project as a utopian demand for a life free of all conflict and pain.[39] He viewed it as yet another attempt to justify the imposition of contrived designs on humanity. Habermas, in Hayek's opinion, laments human "alienation" in capitalist society and condemns the extended order because it "does not satisfy rationalistic criteria of conscious control." Hayek views this as a symptom of the constructivist mentality that tends "to find civilisation unbearable—by definition, as it were."[40]

Wainwright's Critique

Habermas's views have invited a wide diversity of critical responses, not only from Hayek and the "free-market right," but from the left as well. Hilary Wainwright, for instance, criticizes Habermas for not recognizing the resourceful political agency of the worker and student movements.[41] But Wainwright accepts much of Habermas's Critical perspective, including an emphasis on the ideal of a "participatory democracy."

In her book, *Arguments for a New Left: Answering the Free Market Right*, Wainwright examines the resurgence of neoliberalism among the "principled oppositionists in Central and Eastern Europe." Wainwright observes that the anti-authoritarianism of the oppositionists has been profoundly influenced by the "free-market sentiments" of F. A. Hayek.[42] Wainwright focuses specifically on Hayek's critique of "the social engineering state, and its presumption that it is able to know and meet the needs of the people." She roots Hayek's resiliency in his strong "intellectual foundations," and expends considerable energy in debunking the Hayekian worldview.[43] While Wainwright appreciates Hayek's emphasis on tacit, dispersed knowledge, she rejects his assumption that such knowledge "is necessarily exclusively individual in character and cannot provide a basis for collective action."[44] Wainwright believes that Hayekians have appropriated libertarian themes that must be reclaimed by a new left that renounces the social-engineering state, while embracing a vision of democratic self-management.[45] By exploring "the democratization of knowledge," such a new left can transcend the Hayekian strictures of "dogmatic" individualism.[46]

What is striking about Wainwright's analysis is her honesty; she fully admits that the left has failed to respond effectively to Hayek's neoliberalism. Former critiques of Hayek by Wootton and Crosland in the 1940s and 1950s merely reiterated the left's faith in the "benevolent expertise" of technocrats.[47] But Hayek's formidable epistemic arguments were able to survive such critiques. His recognition of the "ephemeral, practical and often tacit" character of knowledge which cannot "even in principle be centralized," is applauded by Wainwright. However, Wainwright rejects the Hayekian assumption that individuals are forever ignorant of the social consequences of their actions.[48]

Wainwright believes that Hayek's arguments are flawed because he denies knowledge "as a social product." She maintains that Hayek's "libertarian starting point" is undermined by an evolutionary view that terminates in a kind of "radical conservatism." His free-market ideal would require a strong government to guard against interest-group pressures for institutional regulation. His "bizarre constitutional proposals," and his conception of capitalism fail to account for the market's "tendencies" toward monopolies and externalities.[49]

And yet, in Wainwright's view, Hayek's antipositivist, antiscientistic premises can "contribute to new foundations for the left." By engaging in a dialogue with Hayekian neoliberalism, the left can sharpen its "conceptual tools," providing a "means through which practical knowledge is socialized, theoretical understanding is scrutinized and partially knowing, collective agents of change are forged."[50]

For Wainwright, Hayek's central error lies in his treatment of knowledge "as an individual attribute, rather than as a social product."[51] In this regard, Wainwright cites, primarily, Hayek's earlier essays on individualism and knowledge. Hayek writes:

> This is the constitutional limitation of man's knowledge and interests, the fact that he *cannot* know more than a tiny part of the whole of society and that therefore all that can enter into his motives are the immediate effects which his actions will have in the sphere he knows. . . . all man's mind can effectively comprehend are the facts of the narrow circle of which he is the center.[52]

Wainwright argues that the significance of this statement lies not in its appreciation of epistemic strictures, but rather, in its assumption that individuals act as "atomistic animals," on the basis of limited knowledge that is

> dogmatically experiential and therefore individual . . . closing off possibilities (rightly) of total rationality and complete knowledge but also (wrongly) of social action to share information and extend the knowledge of individuals through associating for the purpose.[53]

Since knowledge is "a social product," Wainwright argues that "the foundation of Hayek's case for the free market begins to crumble."[54] In searching for an alternative to Hayek, Wainwright surveys theoretical movements such as Critical Theory, Critical Realism, and Postmodernism, all of which can contribute to nonstatist "strategies for transformation" that rely on self-governing, participatory, democratic, and egalitarian institutions. Such new forms must "take account of the tacit, practical character of knowledge," claims Wainwright, thus, subverting the Hayekian argument for unregulated markets. Wainwright seeks to bolster "the genuine possibility and legitimacy of conscious, partially knowing efforts to transform society."[55]

Significantly, Wainwright recognizes the enormous contributions of the Frankfurt school to a reconstruction of the Marxian project. She believes that the Critical theorists have had "the greatest influence" on the new, emerging social movements among workers, women, and students, enabling them to forge "a creative association with Marxism," employing its critical tools for the apprehension of social reality.[56]

Wainwright argues that the social character of knowledge implies that people *can* cooperate, share, and combine their knowledge to overcome their individual epistemic limits, despite their inability to know the social consequences of their actions "in every detail for certain." Since people cannot exercise perfect rationality in the construction and design of social projects, no socialist transformation can depend on strictly "codified" knowledge. A genuine participatory democracy must "utilize practical knowledge and recognize its fallibility."[57]

Following Habermas's psycho-epistemic insights, Wainwright believes that "consciousness-raising groups" within the women's movement can provide a model for grasping tacit elements of knowledge. The women's movement has shown, in Wainwright's view, that the comprehension of tacit, oppressive epistemic and social practices can empower and transform a group of people. Learning to integrate reason and emotion, and to appreciate the tacit character of their domestic skills, women have gained a better understanding of "non-codified forms of knowledge" that provide "a starting-point" for genuine opposition to "the social engineering state."[58]

Like Hayek and the Critical theorists, Wainwright recognizes the instrumentalist basis of social engineering. She states similarly, that the technocratic state

> posits a purely external relationship between ends and means. Ends are given by politicians and means prescribed by technocrats. One implication of this is that there is no conception of self-activity by those who will benefit from the change.[59]

Instrumentalism views the state's actions "as neutral, as if the means chosen do not favour one group over another."[60]

However, according to Wainwright, Hayek gives us "an overly restricted choice" between human fallibility and illusory omniscience. He offers a "hopeless" option between an unregulated market and a centralized, intrusive state. By severing the tie between human intentions and social consequences, Hayek views "accident" as of greater significance to social evolution than human creativity.

In Wainwright's view, since language has a social, historical, and relational character, its "content, distribution and structure" is passed on to individuals intergenerationally.[61] By grasping the social character of knowledge, people can "come closer to achieving their purposes." They can combine dispersed knowledge in an effort to achieve not synoptic omniscience, "but rather a better understanding of the social mechanisms at work, so as to direct their efforts in order that their intentions might be more efficiently fulfilled."[62]

Wainwright's goal is "democratic self-management," or a "participatory democracy" grounded on a "new approach to knowledge."[63] Following the paradigm of "consciousness-raising" in the women's movement, people can embrace "a common sense of purpose and knowledge . . ." Through the integration of individually dispersed knowledge gathered "from any angle," oppressive social structures would become transparent.[64]

Wainwright seeks to replace "historically specific" epistemic notions with "a new approach to social and economic knowledge: one that values and seeks to share its practical dimension while seeking to democratize its theoretical dimension."[65] Toward this end, Wainwright believes that state-supported, "self-managed" cooperatively owned agencies would "gather knowledge of social needs" by examining the "expressions of taste and demand indicated by market trends."

It is fair to assume that Hayek would have categorically rejected such a proposal. Wainwright's state apparatus would intervene significantly; it would regulate income distribution, environmental, health, and safety conditions, labor markets, and the business cycle. Hence, indicative "market trends" would be severely distorted.[66] The "calculation problem" would remain, in Hayek's view, since persistent interference with the market price mechanism would subvert the efficacy of entrepreneurial action.

On a deeper level, however, Wainwright fails to appreciate Hayek's understanding of the *social* character of knowledge. When Hayek argues that knowledge is "essentially dispersed" among individuals in a society, he is not suggesting that individuals are condemned to an epistemic Tower of Babel. The information that can be gathered from a free-flowing price mechanism is useful precisely because it is embedded in a context that takes account of the many, delicate interrelationships between and among various social actors. Individuals can—and do—cooperate under market conditions in which they can evaluate the significance of such information to their individual and collective goals. In Hayek's view the market enables partially knowing individual subjects to interact socially. To posit an end to the market, or violent interference with its network of relative prices, is to posit an end to the very context which gives meaning to articulated and tacit epistemic elements.

Even Wainwright admits that the current social movements that she celebrates have emerged within the wider context provided by market institutions. She recognizes that Hayekians would view these movements as "internal" features of a market society. Nevertheless, she believes that it is possible to combine a highly regulated market with state-funded local agencies that would create "democratic" networks of information-gathering external to the price system.[67] These "democratic" networks would make social actors "more knowing," and hence, "more powerful." Wainwright emphasizes that such a system would require the active financial support of the state to empower those "without private capital," even as it maintains their autonomy.[68]

Wainwright does not suggest the creation of mechanisms which might prevent structural degeneration. She fully recognizes that the agency relationships that she envisions, might degenerate into a form of corporativism, undermining the autonomy of social actors.[69] In such cases, Wainwright's agencies would become "part of the state," pursuing their own parochial interests *undemocratically* within that context.

Despite the problems with Wainwright's proposals, she has provided the left with an explicit response to the Hayekian challenge. Ultimately, however, her recommendations, like those of Habermas, rely heavily on therapeutic means for the articulation of tacit elements of mind. For Hayek, such therapeutic means are limited in their effectiveness. No human psychology is capable of fully articulating the principles that govern the mind. A mind capable of explaining its own cognitive functions is a self-contradiction, for there will always be a cognitive and affective realm that is beyond conscious control.

Furthermore, in Hayek's view, the collective sharing of knowledge cannot eliminate those epistemic strictures that are endemic to the human species. Since society is an organic unity of dynamic, constituent internal relations between and among real individuals, no collective could achieve that which is ontologically and epistemologically impossible to the individuals who compose it.

Within Hayek's spontaneous social order, partially knowing individuals associate and cooperate on a daily basis. It might make for a better world if each individual was increasingly self-reflective. But greater self-knowledge would not eliminate unintended *social* consequences. In Hayek's view, such consequences are so intimately bound up with sociality, that they are constitutive of its very meaning.

And yet, thinkers such as Wainwright and Habermas compel Hayekians to recognize the efficacious possibilities of a radical psychology. A truly radical psychology would not be based on an illusory human omniscience. Rather, it would place the human potential within a realistic cognitive context. It would transcend the dichotomy of reason and emotion, and liberate the troubled human subconscious. The individual would discover the cognitive roots of his or her emotions, while grasping the emotional components of his or her understanding. The individual would recognize that emotions are often the unintended consequences of cognitive development, the products of a spontaneous, split-second evaluational process that takes place within the subconscious mind. Such emotions are not experienced by "design," but can be articulated as a means to the individual's psychological integration. So too, with the creative processes of the mind, a radical psychology would recognize that creativity is a constellation of logic, imagination, intuition, reason, and emotion, with no dichotomy implied between any of its constituents.

Nothing in Hayek's approach should impugn the possibility for such a radical psychology. A spontaneously emergent social movement that promotes psycho-epistemic articulation might very well enable individuals, in their own lives, and in their cooperative efforts with others, to shift the "tacit coefficient of meaning." By comprehending their own thoughts, emotions, and actions, individuals may very well achieve greater self-efficacy.

A movement toward greater self-articulation, however, cannot emerge in a social vacuum. The Hayekian perspective suggests that human action can only be efficacious if it recognizes the context from which it springs and within which it is expressed. The extended, spontaneous order of the market, in Hayek's view, provides the only appropriate context for the emergence of such efficacy. Hayek argues that any excessive tampering with this spontaneous order will undermine the very social mechanisms that generate order. For Hayek "order" is an organic unity in which various elements are internally related such that we may, from the vantage point of any part, form correct expectations concerning the whole.[70] By implication, *dis*order is a state of affairs based on dissolution and systemic degeneration, in which the various elements are fragmented such that it becomes impossible to form any correct expectations. Under such conditions, an infinite number of therapeutic encounters could not possibly generate individual efficacy or social competence.

Still, Hayek's caveat is clear: no radical psychology can propel an individual to the complete mastery of his or her own cognitive processes. And no radical politics can propel a society to the complete mastery of its own destiny. In the light of epistemic strictures and the dialectical critique of utopianism, radicals must answer the perennial question: What is to be done?

Epilogue:
Utopianism and the
Radical Project

On one level, this book has provided a straightforward comparison of the works of Karl Marx and F. A. Hayek, with specific emphasis on their theoretical convergence in the critique of utopianism. But on another level, this book has reconsidered the nature of the radical project. It is my conviction that what makes radical theory *radical* is, partially, its reliance on dialectical methods of inquiry. The critique of utopianism common to both Marx and Hayek, is fundamentally, a critique of *non*dialectical approaches to social theory. Both thinkers view utopianism as founded upon an inadequate method of social theorizing:

1. A utopian theory does not take into account the sociohistorical context of the society within which it is expressed. It puts forth an idealized vision of a new society without recognizing the limits—or the true potential—of existing sociohistorical conditions.
2. A utopian theory does not recognize the internal relationship that exists between the utopian theorist and his or her sociohistorical context. The theorist is internal to the society within which he or she operates, and as such, cannot take a synoptic viewpoint.
3. Utopianism reifies human rationality by abstracting it from the social and historical context on which it genetically depends. Such reification fails to recognize the limits—or the true potential—of human reason.
4. The utopian theorist depends on a constructivist resolution in bridging the gap between theoretical goals and unintended social consequences. Constructivism grants to people an imaginary capacity to construct social institutions as if these were the conscious product of human design, rather than a constellation of human intentions and spontaneously emergent social consequences.

5. The distinction between conscious, purposeful human intentions and unintended social consequences is partially dependent on the distinction between articulate and inarticulate practices and knowledge. Utopianism assumes that the tacit component can be fully articulated, leading to the complete triumph of conscious human agency.

Based on this description of utopian theorizing, it is apparent that both Marx and Hayek are anti-utopian in many significant ways. Marx's approach, like Hayek's, is founded on a concern for social and historical specificity. Both thinkers recognize the internal relationship between the theorist and his or her context. They view rationality as a distinctly human capacity that cannot be abstracted from the social and historical conditions within which it is expressed. They agree that no individual can achieve a synoptic view of the whole, and that the individual's conditions of existence are partly constitutive of his or her identity. Moreover, both Marx and Hayek recognize the distinction between conscious human agency and unintended social consequences. They condemn as utopian any attempt to construct new social institutions since these are spontaneously emergent. For both thinkers a recognition of contextual limitations is simultaneously an acknowledgment of real potential.

In their convergent criticisms of utopianism, both Marx and Hayek uphold the integrity of radical, dialectical methods of inquiry. Hayek would agree wholeheartedly with Marx's observation: "To be radical is to grasp things by the root."[1] Social theory, for both thinkers, must be based on a fundamental commitment to this truth. To be radical, in this methodological sense, is to be dialectical, to search for roots, to recognize the organic unity and internal relations of the social totality, and to view social change as immanent to its context, the potential for transformation emerging spontaneously from within, rather than imposed from without. By contrast, to be utopian is to be nondialectical, to assume an illusory, synoptic vantage point on the social totality, and to construct an ahistorical, acontextual ideal society based on a pretense of knowledge.

To reject utopian theorizing does not imply the rejection of those progressive goals of peace, freedom, and dignity that utopian theory often acknowledges as its own. Hayek was the first to admit that on questions of value he shared much with his socialist adversaries.[2]

The prime difference between Marx and Hayek is not ethical or political, but epistemological. Though both thinkers recognize the organic link between goals and context, between potentiality and actuality, they differ in their comprehension of the nature of epistemic limitations. Whereas Hayek views the strictures on human knowledge as tacit and existentially limiting, Marx views them as historically specific to precommunist social formations. Marx—and his Critical successors—suggest a resolution in which human agency triumphs over unintended social consequences through the full articulation and integration of tacit and dispersed knowledge.

In his more constrained assessment of human cognitive potential, Hayek did not intend to extinguish the radical hope for a better society. Nevertheless, he claimed that he often smiled when reading the concluding chapters of books written by evolutionists, who, having conceded the spontaneous, emergent qualities of social evolution,

> call on human reason . . . to seize the reins and control future development . . . The idea that reason, itself created in the course of evolution, should now be in a position to determine its own future evolution . . . is inherently contradictory.[3]

Paradoxically, however, even Hayek conceded that there was a certain power inherent in utopian exhortations. Hayek was crucially aware of the need to uplift the human imagination. He viewed politics as "the art of the possible," and political philosophy as "the art of making politically possible the seemingly impossible."[4]

For Hayek, political inspiration is the sole, legitimate function of utopianism. Utopia "is a bad word today," in Hayek's view, because most utopian models are beset by "internal contradictions." Anchored in social reality and cognizant of existential conditions, a critical, "internally consistent" ideal can offer a "guiding conception" for political change. Such an ideal is an "indispensable precondition" of any rational social policy. Thus, according to Hayek, the realization of radical, progressive goals will ultimately depend on the achievement of "an effective framework" within which there can emerge a fully "functioning spontaneous order."[5] In what Kukathas has characterized aptly, as a "*constructivist* turn in Hayek's thought,"[6] the anti-utopian Hayek writes:

> We must make the building of a free society once more an intellectual adventure, a deed of courage. What we lack is a liberal Utopia, a programme which seems neither a mere defense of things as they are nor a diluted kind of socialism, but a truly liberal radicalism which does not spare the susceptibilities of the

mighty . . . which is not too severely practical and which does not confine itself to what appears today as politically possible. We need intellectual leaders who are prepared to resist the blandishments of power and influence and who are willing to work for an ideal, however small may be the prospects of its early realization. They must be men who are willing to stick to principle and to fight for their full realization however remote. . . . The main lesson which the true liberal must learn from the success of the socialists is that it was their courage to be Utopian which gained them the support of the intellectuals and thereby an influence on public opinion which is daily making possible what only recently seemed utterly remote. . . . Unless we can make the philosophic foundations of a free society once more a living intellectual issue, and its implementation a task which challenges the ingenuity and imagination of our liveliest minds, the prospects of freedom are indeed dark. But if we can regain that belief in the power of ideas which was the mark of liberalism at its best, the battle is not lost.[7]

As a genuinely dialectical theorist, Hayek grasps that every critical moment of inquiry must contain within it a positive anticipation of a revolutionary alternative. Hayek would maintain, however, that such a revolutionary alternative need not be Marxist in its substantive orientation. Despite their common anti-utopianism, both Hayek and Marx, to differing degrees, project a "constructivist" ideal to complete our understanding of what it means to be "radical." For Hayek, that ideal is antistatist and nonauthoritarian. Hayek merges a dialectical sensibility with a substantive recognition of epistemic strictures and real potentials, human freedom, the rule of law, and the unfettered market. But Hayek provides little guidance as to how such a libertarian ideal could be realized. His many critics are correct to note that this ideal will not necessarily emerge from the spontaneous, evolutionary traditions, customs, and morals that Hayek celebrates.

Still, Hayek's greatest contribution to the radical cause lies in his recognition of epistemic strictures. On this basis, Hayek challenges the new radicals to promote a more realistic vision of social change. If utopian ideals are to have any useful function in social theory, they must inspire people to reach for all that is within their grasp by stretching the limits of the human potential.

There is some evidence that certain thinkers, on both the socialist left and the libertarian right, are beginning to examine the central question: To what extent do the strictures on human knowledge preclude rational, efficacious, social action? Despite the differences among them, and regardless of the success of their respective endeavors, such thinkers recognize that partially knowing human actors, living under concrete social and historical conditions, can achieve efficacy in their lives by shifting the tacit dimensions of mind toward greater articulation.[8] Out of this movement can emerge the possibility for radical, social transformation.

By gaining a deeper understanding of the dialectical relationship between goals and context, future generations of radical thinkers might pave the way for progressive alternatives to the status quo, alternatives that are rooted in *viable*, if distant, possibilities, and that uplift the human imagination without endangering the survival of the species.

Notes

Introduction

1. Marx (24 January 1873), "Afterword to the second German edition," in Marx ([1867] 1967):20.

2. Lukács (March 1919), "What is Orthodox Marxism?," in Lukács (1971):1-2.

3. Some of the following was developed in conjunction with Sciabarra (1995).

4. Aristotle, *Rhetoric* [1.2.1355b26-27], in Aristotle (1941):1329. In this context, "dialectics" also suggests a type of metaphysical reasoning from first principles. Thanks to Douglas B. Rasmussen in Kelley (1993) for this observation.

5. Nevertheless, Irwin [(1988):174-78] argues that Aristotle uses a form of dialectic in negative demonstration, in which one proceeds from premises that one's opponent cannot reject. This "strong dialectic" is an aspect of Aristotle's defense of "first principles" or ultimate truths. Thanks to Douglas B. Rasmussen for bringing this to my attention in a personal correspondence (19 April 1994).

6. Engels ([1878] 1947):29, 29n. See also Marx ([1867] 1967):59, 408.

7. Lenin (1914-16), "On Aristotle's *Metaphysics*," in Selsam and Martel (1963):361.

8. In the history of philosophy, it was not Hegel who enunciated the triadic formulation. One can find hints of this terminology in Kant's discussion of the antinomies, but it is used most extensively by Fichte ([1794] 1970).

9. There are many defenses of the continuity in Marx's thought. See for instance, Ollman (1976):xiv-xvi; Kolakowski (1978):263; McCarthy (1990):3.

10. So too, some of Hayek's critics have tended to focus on single strands of his thought, mistaking the part for the whole. Thus, as I argue in

Chapter Seven, Wainwright (1994) is quick to characterize Hayek as a "dogmatic" individualist, without recognizing his broader, dialectical method.

11. Traditionally, the Frankfurt School has been identified with phenomenological Marxism. See Jay (1973). Althusser is chief among the more structuralist interpreters. See Althusser and Balibar ([1970] 1971).

12. See Ollman (1976); (1979); (1993); Gould (1978); Meikle (1985); Brien (1987).

13. Marx ([1867] 1967):19.

14. To say that each audience has its own interests is not to imply the doctrine of polylogism, that is, that each group (e.g., class, nation, race, etc.) has its own distinctive "logic." Rather, each audience has a specific vantage point that must be taken into account in the presentation of one's ideas. For a superb critique of polylogism, see Mises ([1949] 1963):72-91; ([1957] 1969):31.

15. Ollman (1979):150.

16. Ibid., 121. Ollman's interpretation encompasses many other aspects in Marx's method: Marx's ontological view of internal relations; his four interlocking processes that constitute his epistemology (perception, abstraction, conception, and orientation); his method of intellectual reconstruction; and his distinctive method of inquiry, which traces relations in their interdependence. Ollman [(1976):97] also mentions "praxis" as the distinctive means of human appropriation. See Ollman (1979); (1993), especially Chapter two.

17. See, for instance, Kamenka in Marx [(1983):xliv-xlv] who believes that Engels was "the true founder of 'Marxism,'" suggesting that Engels reconstructed Marx's theory into a "religion" of positivistic-mechanistic "orthodoxy." It is true that Engels employs a "dialectics of nature," but I do not utilize any of these theories in this book.

Chapter 1

1. Plamenatz (1975):vii.

2. Popper ([1962a] 1971):167-68.

3. Kirk ([1953] 1986):45.

4. Hayek ([1956b] 1967):222.

5. Hayek (1960):400.

6. Hayek (1944):199.

7. Hayck ([1976] 1978):296.

8. Nisbet (1980):2.

9. East (1980):35.

10. Paradoxically, Marx saw in Burke *both* conservatism *and* liberalism. He viewed Burke as "an out and out vulgar bourgeois. . . . [who] always sold himself in the best market" whether he was "in the pay of the English oligarchy" as an opponent of the French Revolution, or "in the pay of the North American colonies" where he "played the Liberal against the English oligarchy." See Marx ([1867] 1967):760n.

11. Burke ([1790] 1955):29.

12. Barber (1986):15. I recognize that there are many interpretive difficulties in Locke scholarship. In this regard, see especially Vaughn (1980*a*); (1980*b*). Interestingly, Kukathas observes that several scholars, such as Avineri and Pelczynski, consider the works of Locke, Hume, Smith, and Ferguson as the inspiration for Hegel's view of civil society as a system of interdependence. See Kukathas (1989):208.

13. Hartz (1955):50. For a provocative application of the Hartzian insights, see Roelofs (1976). It is Roelofs's book that first alerted me to a problematic dichotomy between theory and practice in radical politics. Roelofs's approach emphasizes the "ideology" and "myth" that have crippled radical efforts to fundamentally transform American institutions.

14. Barry (1982):22-24.

15. Hayck (1973):10.

16. Hayek ([1970] 1978):20.

17. Hayek (1976):25.

18. Popper ([1962*a*] 1971):167.

19. My interpretation of the dialectical similarities between Hayek and Marx is distinct, but others have noted certain parallels. Some scholars, like G. B. Madison, have cited approvingly, my own view that Hayek endorsed a doctrine of internal relations. See Madison (1990):44; 53 n.10. Others, like John Gray (1980), have suggested previously that Hayek's method, like Marx's, is comparable to historicism.

20. For example, see Lukes (1968) who criticizes Popper and Hayek as methodological individualists. An interesting contrast is provided by Therborn [(1984):354-55] who views the modern evolutionist perspective as a "conservative" counterpart to the Frankfurt School. Nevertheless, Therborn's characterization of Hayek's thought as "reactionary" is a gross distortion.

21. Hayek ([1952] 1976); (1948).

22. Wainwright (1994):5. I will discuss Wainwright's critique in the final chapter of this book.

23. Wainwright cites Hayek (1944); (1948); (1960); (1988). Absent are any analyses of Hayek ([1967] 1980); (1973); (1976); ([1978] 1985); (1981).

24. Nishiyama, "Introduction," in Hayek (1984):lv.

25. Ibid., liv.

26. Madison has argued persuasively that Hayek's self-characterization as a "methodological individualist" was primarily a political "counterpose" to the predominating "socialist" and "collectivist" tendencies in modern social science. For Madison, "the ultimate meaning of Hayek's 'individualism' . . . is that people can exist as *individuals* only to the degree that they exist as members of *communities* . . ." See Madison (1990):46, 51.

27. An anonymous reviewer of the current study made such an observation.

28. Popper ([1962*b*] 1971):93.

29. Hayek (1967):76-77.

30. Ibid., 77.

31. Hayek ([1943] 1948):71.

32. Hayek (1967):70-71.

33. Polanyi ([1958] 1962):381. Polanyi's insights into the tacit dimensions of knowledge, explored in Chapter Three, are crucial to the Hayekian critique of utopianism.

34. Hayek ([1933] 1991):27.

35. Lavoie has made a similar observation on the relationship between Austrian economics and contemporary hermeneutics. He sees hermeneutics as the "missing link" in the modern American-Austrian movement. "It reconnects Austrians to their roots in the German language from which their English language training in economics had been artificially disconnected." See Lavoie in Lavoie (1991):25. While I do not discuss the hermeneutic tradition to any great extent in the current study, it should be noted that dialectics is *basic* to the hermeneutical approach. It is also significant that Aristotle is considered the father of dialectical inquiry; there are important intellectual links between the early Austrian school and Aristotelian realism. See Chapter Six, n.38.

36. Hayek ([1933] 1991):27.

37. Hayek (1988):9.

38. See Gotthelf (1976), "Aristotle's conception of final causality," in Gotthelf and Lennox (1987):230.

39. Popper ([1962*b*] 1971):226.

40. Hegel ([1807] 1977):2.

41. This is not to imply that organicism and atomism are the *only* two theories of social relationships. But most contemporary approaches are variations on either organic or atomist, internalist or externalist, dialectical or dualistic principles. Much of this section was developed in conjunction with Sciabarra (1987).

42. Hellman (1979):161.

43. Hook ([1936] 1950):62.

44. Kelley (1986):81.

45. Ibid., 168.

46. Nietzsche [[1883-85] (1905):132] decries the "*immaculate* perception of all things."

47. Kelley maintains that perception is the joint product of the specific sense modalities in use, the object itself, and the material context within which we perceive (e.g., through air, in water, etc.). None of this should be interpreted as a conflation of the mode of awareness and the object of awareness. Kelley, true to his realist roots, and in the tradition of Ayn Rand's Objectivist philosophy, argues that awareness is inherently relational, that is, that consciousness is consciousness of objects that exist independently of the means by which human beings acquire knowledge. See Kelley (1986); Rand (1990).

48. Ollman and Vernoff (1986):xiii.

49. It is beyond the scope of the current study to defend the proposition that the dialectical method is valid, or that dualism as such, is invalid. While this study identifies a necessary link between radicalism and dialectics, it does not engage in a philosophical defense of the ultimate validity of the dialectical method. Such a task would require at the very least, a full justification of internal relations based on a contextualist epistemology. I touch on some of these issues in Sciabarra (1995).

50. The vast philosophical issues underlying the problem of dualism were first brought to my attention by Wolf Heydebrand. Heydebrand [(1981):92] identifies different forms of dualism. He maintains that in each form of dualism there is "an absolute duality of the principles that govern

reality" since the two spheres are viewed as "mutually irreducible meta-physical substances or forces." Thus,

> ontological dualism posits the dichotomy of matter and mind, moral and religious dualism the radical separateness of good and evil, epistemological dualism that of the real object and the datum immediately present to the knowing mind.

It should be emphasized here, that I use the phrase, "dualistic methodology," in a manner which differs from the phrase, "methodological dualism," as employed by the Austrian economist, Ludwig von Mises. Mises argues that there are methodological differences between the study of the physical world and the study of human action. He believes that the appropriation of physical science techniques by social science constitutes scientism. Hence, it is an illegitimate transference of methodology. See Chapter Two for a brief discussion of Hayek's early thought which characterized constructivist rationality as scientistic. On Mises's praxeological method, see Mises ([1949] 1963); ([1957] 1969).

51. The finest expositor of libertarian dualism is Murray Rothbard. See Rothbard ([1970] 1977); (1978b). I criticize this form of libertarian dualism in Sciabarra (1987); (1988a).

52. Ollman (1993):11.

53. Blanshard (1962):475. Brien [(1987):215, n.19] observes correctly that "when Blanshard speaks about 'the nature of a term,' he refers both to the nature of an individual as grasped in thought and language and to the nature of an individual as it exists concretely." See Blanshard (1940, v.2):484.

54. Blanshard (1940, v.2):452.

55. Blanshard (1962):481.

56. Ibid., 482.

57. Ibid., 485.

58. Hayek (1981):155.

59. Hayek ([1946] 1948):6-7.

60. Hayek (1988):21.

61. Ibid., 12.

62. Hayek (1981):155.

63. Hayek ([1965] 1967):86-87.

64. For a more detailed treatment of Hayek's opposition to strict moral relativism, see Gray (1984):56-58; Diamond (1980).

65. Hayek (1976):26.

66. Gray (1984):57.

67. Hayek (1976):26-27.

68. Hayek (1988):8.

69. Hayek ([1964] 1967):38.

70. Blanshard (1940, v.2):446.

71. Ibid., 451.

Chapter 2

1. Hayek (1988):6.

2. Hayek (1973):36.

3. Hayek ([1968a] 1978):73.

4. Hayek (1988):74.

5. Popper ([1962b] 1971):93.

6. Elster (1985); and Karl Polanyi in Popper ([1962b] 1971):323n. Karl Polanyi (1886-1964) is not to be confused with his brother, Michael Polanyi (1891-1976), whose works I discuss in conjunction with the distinction between articulate and inarticulate knowledge. Interesting parallels can also be drawn between the notion of "unintended consequences" in social theory and the implications of "the new science" of "chaos theory." See Lemieux (1994).

7. Bartley (1984):27.

8. Ricoeur ([1971] 1977):324-26.

9. See Friedman (1962); Kolko (1963); Lowi ([1969] 1979); Hayek (1944). Another useful volume of revisionist history is Radosh and Rothbard (1972), which includes essays from authors on the socialist left and the libertarian right, united in their assessment of the growth of the "Leviathan" state.

10. Hayek [([1965] 1967):83] cites Gladstone as the first person to use the term "constructivism" to describe the "engineering type of mind."

11. Ibid.

12. Hayek (1981):129; (1988).

13. Hayek ([1965] 1967):93.

14. In this regard, see Kukathas (1989):208-10. Kukathas notes correctly that Hayek is inconsistent—or unclear—in his application of the "constructivist" label, especially with regard to such thinkers as Hegel, Marx, Vico, Mandeville, Hume, Ferguson, Smith, Humboldt, Kant, Locke, John Stuart Mill, and Spencer. I agree wholeheartedly with Kukathas's view that Hegel and Marx did *not* see society as the product of conscious design, and that Hayek is wrong to excoriate these thinkers as fully constructivistic.

15. Hayek ([1965] 1967):94.

16. Hayek (1988):21.

17. Ibid., 8.

18. See for instance, Hayek ([1952] 1976).

19. Hayek ([1967] 1980):viii.

20. Hayek (1988):66.

21. Jay (1973):81.

22. Gray (1984):52.

23. See Vaughn (1982):9. See also Gray (1984); Butler (1983); Hayek (1960); ([1962a] 1967); (1973); (1981); (1988). Gray calls Hayek's approach a variant of "systems utilitarianism."

24. Barry (1982):46.

25. Rothbard (1987):3. In the current study, I do not critique Rothbard's analysis of Hayek. A Hayekian might respond that even if Rothbard is correct to note the class character of government interventionism, it does not follow that the overall growth of government has been *intended* by the various classes. It is still quite possible to see the overall growth of the state as an unintended consequence of the relative expansion of particular government agencies, programs, and regulations. Thanks to Karen Vaughn for this particular insight.

26. Wainwright (1994):56.

27. Tomlinson [(1990):54] argues that this dualism is even at the heart of Hayek's distinction between "critical" and "constructivist" rationalism.

28. Hayek (1981):140.

Chapter 3

1. Lavoie [(1982):21-22] expresses a provocative insight when he writes:"Both Marx and Mises pointed out that rationality as we know it is

itself a product of the emergence of market relations." Mises, the father of modern Austrian economics, was Hayek's mentor. The view that rationality is internal to capitalism is one held by thinkers as diverse as Marx, Mises, Weber, and Ayn Rand.

2. Hayek (1981):176.

3. Caputo (1988):5.

4. Shaffer ([1975] 1976):14.

5. See Aristotle *Physics* 3.4-5.204a34-206a7 in Aristotle (1941):260-64. Also see Rand (1990):148-49.

6. The issue of cognitive efficacy has been discussed at length in the works of the psychologist Nathaniel Branden. See Branden (1969); (1971); (1983). Branden relies heavily on the works of Ayn Rand, who explored the interrelationships between epistemology and politics. See Sciabarra (1989); (1995). Also see Childs (1974) who applies Branden's theory of psychological efficacy to a study of statist interventionism.

7. Hayek ([1945] 1948):78.

8. Hayek's distinction between "critical" and "constructivist" rationalism resembles Popper's distinction between "true" and "pseudo" rationalism. In Popper's words, "true rationalism" shows "an awareness of one's limitations, the intellectual modesty of those who know how often they err, and how much they depend on others even for this knowledge. It is the realization that we must not expect too much from reason." Like Hayek, Popper also calls this "critical rationalism." By contrast, "pseudo-rationalism" shows an "immodest belief in one's superior intellectual gifts, the claim to be initiated, to know with certainty and with authority." It is the belief in reason as an "infallible instrument of discovery." See Popper ([1962b] 1971):227.

9. Hayek ([1945] 1948):80.

10. Hayek ([1970] 1978):8-9.

11. Hayek ([1962b] 1967):43. The Sapir quote is taken from, "The Unconscious Patterning of Behaviour in Society," (1927) in *Selected Writings of Edward Sapir*, edited by D. G. Mandelbaum, University of Chicago Press, 1949.

12. Hayek (1981):157.

13. Polanyi ([1958] 1962):56.

14. Hayek ([1968a] 1978):81.

15. Polanyi ([1958] 1962):250.

16. Thanks to Karen Vaughn for this observation.

17. Hayek (1973):14.

18. Hayek ([1962*b*] 1967):62. See also Hayek ([1952] 1976):188-89.

19. Hayek ([1964] 1967):39.

20. Kukathas (1989):54.

21. Hayek ([1933] 1991):19.

22. Tomlinson (1990):107, 147. See also Wootton (1945):66, n.1; Crosland (1957):500.

23. Blanshard (1940, v.2):455-56.

24. Ibid., 489.

25. Hayek in Geddes (1979):D1.

26. Hayek (1961):28.

27. Popper ([1962*a*] 1971):167-68.

28. Hayek ([1956*a*] 1967):130.

29. Sciabarra (1995) argues that Rand is the first libertarian thinker to attempt such a grand synthesis.

30. Hayek (1960):69-70.

Chapter 4

1. Marx and Engels ([1848] 1968):49.

2. Marx ([1843-44] 1967):247.

3. Marx ([1857-58] 1973):83.

4. Marx ([1894] 1967):817; ([1863*a*] 1963):393.

5. Ollman (1976):61. Hook [([1936] 1950):63] observes that in Marx's theory, the part is the abstraction, the whole is the concrete.

6. Marx ([1846] 1982):36.

7. Ibid., 38.

8. Engels ([1878] 1947):408-09.

9. Engels ([1880] 1968):379.

10. An interesting discussion of the utopian socialists is provided by Kolakowski (1978):187-214.

11. Plamenatz (1975):409-10; 455. Plamenatz distinguishes between the "rebel," the "reformer," the "non-revolutionary Utopian," and the "revolutionary" as "ideal types." Significantly, he criticizes Marx's "claim to be scientific and not Utopian," as "shoddy and evasive." See Plamenatz (1975):472.

12. Marx ([1857-58] 1973):885.

13. Marx ([1894] 1967):175.

14. Thomas (1980):56.

15. Ibid., 348, 348n. On the distinction between logical and relational contradiction, see the next chapter. Interestingly, a debate within modern libertarianism echoes the debate between Marxists and anarchists. Libertarian anarchists like Murray Rothbard, endorse an antagonistic distinction between state and market. By contrast, Ayn Rand condemned such anarchism as a "naive, floating abstraction." Like Marx, Rand saw anarchism and statism as two sides of the same coin. See Rand (1964):107-15. For a critique of libertarian dualism, see Sciabarra (1987); (1988a).

16. Marcuse (1972):51-52.

17. Marx ([1867] 1967):356.

18. Marx ([1865] 1982):145.

19. Marx ([1868b] 1982):201; ([1867] 1967):17.

20. Marx ([1885] 1967):16.

21. Marx ([1877] 1982):290.

22. Marx ([1875] 1968):333-34.

23. Marx ([1843] 1963):44.

24. Marx ([1843-44] 1967):240.

25. Ibid., 236.

26. Ibid., 225, 231.

27. Marx ([1842] 1967):137-38.

28. Marx and Engels ([1848] 1968):60.

29. Engels ([1878] 1947):324n, 311. Engels writes, concerning the bourgeois French revolutionaries of the eighteenth century, that their goal was the creation of a "rational government," a "rational society." For these rev-

olutionaries, "everything that ran counter to eternal *reason* was to be remorsely done away with." Commenting on the Reign of Terror, Engels [([1880] 1968):402] observes:"The state based upon reason completely collapsed."

30. Lichtheim ([1964] 1982):55.

31. Engels ([1885] 1982):362.

32. Sayer (1983):161. Sayer explains that within Marx's method, "we cannot properly say that individuals *create* society which in turn creates them, for the simple reason that at any point the existence of either presupposes . . . the other."

33. Engels ([1890*b*] 1982):395.

34. Engels ([1895*a*] 1982):455. Engels [([1886] 1968):622-23], comparing nature and society, emphasizes that in human society, "nothing happens without a conscious purpose, without an intended aim" but that because of conflicting human wills, society resembles "the realm of unconscious nature" and its "blind" forces.

35. Elster (1985):3-4.

36. Elster (1986):38, 194. Godelier [(1972):352-53] observes similarly, that unintended social consequences are the basis of every internal contradiction in capitalism. Contradiction appears

> without anyone wishing to make it appear. This contradiction is therefore *unintentional*. It is a result of the action of all the agents of the system and of the development of the system itself, and is never the project of any consciousness, is never anyone's goal.

37. Meek (1954):92, 107. On the issue of unintended social consequences, Elster has suggested too, a convergence between Marx and such thinkers as Mandeville, Smith, Ferguson, *and* Hegel. To his credit, Elster refers the reader specifically to Hayek's essay on "The results of human action but not of human design," reprinted in Hayek ([1967] 1980):96-105. See Elster (1985):4, n.1.

38. Flacks (1982):16.

39. Marx ([1857-58] 1973):161.

40. Marx (1976):24.

41. Marx ([1857-58] 1973):196-97.

42. Marx ([1894] 1967):807.

43. Marx ([1863c] 1971):271-72.

44. Marx ([1867] 1967):508.

45. Engels ([1884] 1968):577-83.

46. Marx ([1867] 1967):106.

47. Marx ([1863c] 1971):288-89.

48. Marx ([1863a] 1963):409.

49. Marx ([1867] 1967):363.

50. Marx ([1844] 1964):108.

51. In Chapter Six, I address the distinction between knowledge and labor as it relates to Marx's vision for social transformation.

52. Marx ([1857-58] 1973):148, 146.

53. Ibid., 200.

54. Ibid., 496.

55. Ibid., 652.

56. Hayek (1988):82.

57. Draper (1977):506.

58. Marx ([1844a] 1967):349.

59. Marx and Engels ([1845-46] 1970):53.

60. Ibid., 53.

61. Marx ([1863c] 1971):443. Marx recognized science as a force of material production, which, like others in capitalism, was subject to the same historical limitations. But it was the Frankfurt school's critique of scientism that propelled Marxist thought to a deeper level of understanding in this area. I will explore some of these themes in Chapter Seven.

62. Marx and Engels ([1845-46] 1970):64.

63. Marx ([1859] 1970):21.

64. Ibid., 105, 114.

65. Marx ([1857-58] 1973):99.

66. Ibid., 278.

Chapter 5

1. Among the opponents of Marxism who view the materialist conception of history as strict technological determinism, there are: Acton ([1955] 1973); Mises ([1957] 1969); Rand (1961).

2. Alexander (1982*b*):299. Elster [(1983):158] has argued too, that Marx's viewpoint constitutes "not only an economic, but a technological conception of history." Elster concludes, however, that the Marxist conception is teleological. I will discuss Marx's historical resolution in greater detail later in this chapter and in Chapter Six.

3. Avineri (1968); Ollman (1976); Giddens (1979).

4. Alexander (1982*a*):125.

5. Engels ([1890*b*] 1982):396. See also Kolakowski (1978):370.

6. For a fuller discussion of the difference between asymmetric, causal, and reciprocal relations, especially in Marx's social ontology, see Gould (1978):89, 92, 184, n.22. See also Bottomore (1983).

7. Marx ([1857-58] 1973):83.

8. Marx and Engels ([1845-46] 1970):42.

9. Marx ([1844] 1964):137.

10. Ibid., 182.

11. Marx ([1868*a*] 1982):196-97.

12. Marx and Engels ([1845-46] 1970):51.

13. Among the Hayekian-influenced critics of Marxism, Sowell presents a sympathetic rendering of Marx's rejection of both mechanistic materialism and idealism. See Sowell (1985):36-52.

14. Marx ([1844] 1964):145.

15. Marx and Engels ([1845-46] 1970):47.

16. Ibid., 83.

17. Marx ([1845] 1967):400-02.

18. Marx ([1844] 1964):113.

19. Marx ([1867] 1967):177.

20. Marx ([1844] 1964):140.

21. Marx ([1867] 1967):178.

22. See Chapter Two.

23. Hayek ([1962*b*] 1967):62.

24. Marx ([1847] 1967):480.

25. Engels ([1878] 1947):200-01.

26. Marx ([1857-58] 1973):98.

27. Interestingly, modern libertarians argue the same point. Rothbard claims that the state is an epiphenomenon of the market because it is genetically dependent on social production. The state expropriates wealth. It also appropriates the spontaneously emergent legal and judicial institutions of the market order. For an introduction to Rothbard's political thought, see Rothbard (1978*b*). Also see Sciabarra (1988*a*):147-240.

28. Marx ([1867] 1967):713.

29. Ibid., 742.

30. Ibid., 754-62.

31. Marx ([1879] 1982):299.

32. Marx ([1894] 1967):196. See also Avineri (1968):252.

33. Marx ([1867] 1967):9.

34. The following, brief exploration of Austrian theory obscures the complexities of the analysis. Hayek, Mises, and Rothbard develop Austrian insights with great sophistication. See Hayek ([1929] 1966); ([1931] 1967); (1978); Mises ([1912] 1971); ([1949] 1963); Rothbard ([1963] 1975); (1970); ([1970] 1977); ([1976] 1980); (1978*a*). Rothbard's works in particular, focus on the class dimensions of the business cycle.

35. For an excellent discussion of Marx's monetary theory, and its similarity to Austrian-school economics, see Vorhies (1989).

36. See Hayek (1978) for a provocative proposal for the "denationalization" of money and credit.

37. Marx ([1894] 1967):493.

38. Marx ([1859] 1970):119, 148.

39. Marx ([1894] 1967):362.

40. Ibid., 490.

41. Marx ([1863*c*] 1971):507.

42. Engels ([1890a] 1982):393. This theory has been called the "dialectical materialist" conception of history. But McLellan ([1971] 1980:152, n.2) explains that "dialectical materialism" was a descriptive phrase first used by Joseph Dietzgen in the 1870s. It was later popularized by the Russian Marxist, Plekhanov.

43. Engels ([1890c] 1982):397; ([1894] 1982):441.

44. Marx ([1863a] 1963):288.

45. Marx ([1894] 1967):791-92.

46. Ollman (1976):273-74; (1993):133-46; Althusser (1971). Althusser attempts to trace the different "respective indices of effectivity" within the base-superstructure interrelation. He argues that different aspects of the superstructure have different effects, even though these are determined "in the last instance" by the material base. Althusser [(1971):129-30] claims that there are varying degrees of relative autonomy of the superstructure and "reciprocal action" on the base. See also, Poulantzas [(1978):16], who objects to the "constructivist image of 'base' and 'superstructure' which . . . cannot in fact provide a correct representation of the articulation of social reality."

47. Popper ([1940] 1963).

48. Despite his mischaracterization of dialectics, Popper must be credited with genuinely grasping the complex interrelationships in Marx's theory. Popper [([1962b] 1971):100] argues correctly that the economistic reading of Marx is a gross misinterpretation.

49. Novack ([1969] 1971):17. See also, Hunt (1950):17-23.

50. Aristotle, *Metaphysics* [4.3.1005b18-21] in Aristotle (1941):736.

51. Ollman (1976):19.

52. Kolakowski (1978):1.

53. See McCarthy (1990); (1992).

54. Marcuse ([1941] 1960):42.

55. Meikle (1985):36.

56. Hegel ([1812-16] 1969):107. See also, editor's note in Marx ([1844] 1964):57-58.

57. Hegel ([1807] 1977):2.

58. Meikle (1985):118-19.

59. See Hook ([1936] 1950); Marcuse ([1941] 1960); Bernstein (1971); Gould (1978); Meikle (1985); Copleston (1985); McCarthy (1990); (1992).

Copleston [(1985):334] also notes the common epistemological and ontological realism of Marxist and Thomistic philosophy. See also Sciabarra
(1990).

60. Marx ([1867] 1967):408, 59. Interestingly, Popper believes that
Marxism owes more to the Platonic, rather than the Aristotelian, tradition.
Popper views Plato, Hegel, and Marx as the true enemies of the "open society." For Popper, Aristotle's influence on Hegel and Marx is merely a derivative of Platonism. Popper does not view Aristotle as an original thinker.
See Popper ([1962a], [1962b] 1971):1. Like Popper, Hayek believes that the
Aristotelian legacy is a mixed blessing. Hayek [([1965] 1967):94] acknowledges Aristotle, Cicero, and St. Thomas Aquinas as pivotal figures in the formulation of critical, rather than constructivist, rationalism. But Hayek
[(1988):143, 47] denigrates Aristotle for his ignorance of evolution. Aristotelianism is also criticized as "the foundation of socialist thought." Unlike
Marx, Hayek does not formally recognize that many of his own methodological presuppositions contain dynamic, dialectical elements first presented in the works of Aristotle. However, these Aristotelian methodological elements were explicit in the early Austrian school, particularly in the
works of Menger and Boehm-Bawerk. See Chapter Six, n.38.

61. Aristotle, *Metaphysics*, in Aristotle (1941):681-926; Copleston
([1946] 1985):304.

62. Aristotle, *De Anima* (*On the Soul*), [2.2.414a16-28], in Aristotle
(1941):558-59.

63. Aristotle, *De Partibus Animalium* (*On the Parts of Animals*),
[1.5.645a31-37 and 2.1.646a27-29], in Aristotle (1941):657, 659.

64. Heilbroner (1987):8. Heilbroner's essay is derived from his book,
Marxism:For and Against (1981). Of course, Heilbroner has merely expanded
on Hegel's distinction between the "lord" and the "bondsman." See Hegel
([1807] 1977):115-19. It should be noted too, that Aristotle saw "master"
and "slave" as "correlatives." See Aristotle, *Categories* [7.761-19], in Aristotle (1941):20.

65. Marx ([1847] 1976):32-33.

66. Meikle (1985):165.

67. See Meikle (1985). Interestingly, whereas Meikle sees Marx's historical teleology as an outgrowth of his "Aristotelianism," Elster [(1986):22]
views Marx as a "transitional figure" in nineteenth-century social thought,
who had broken from the traditional theological approaches, only to retain
their teleological elements. Habermas [([1976] 1979):141] also recognizes
that historical materialism can exhibit teleological elements. I discuss
Habermas's reconstruction of historical materialism in Chapter Seven. For
another view—and defense—of historical materialism, see Cohen (1978).

68. Ollman (1993):137.

69. Ibid., 143-44.

70. Marx ([1845] 1967):402.

71. Marx ([1844] 1964):141.

Chapter 6

1. Marx ([1867] 1967):10.

2. Marx ([1875] 1968):323.

3. Marx ([1863b] 1968):117-18.

4. Marx and Engels ([1845-46] 1970):61.

5. Marx ([1871] 1983):532.

6. Marx and Engels ([1844] 1967):394-95.

7. Engels ([1893] 1982):438-39.

8. Marx ([1859] 1970):21.

9. Engels ([1878] 1947):340-41.

10. Engels ([1891] 1968):262.

11. Marx and Engels ([1848] 1968):48, 52.

12. Engels [([1894] 1968):644] maintains that small peasants would be exempted from statist expropriation, which is reserved for big landowners.

13. Marx and Engels ([1848] 1968):52-53.

14. Marx ([1857-58] 1973):651.

15. Hayek (1954):28.

16. Engels ([1881b] 1982):320.

17. Engels ([1884] 1968):589.

18. Marx ([1875] 1968):324-25, 331.

19. Marx and Engels ([1848] 1968):53.

20. Marx ([1844b] 1967):281.

21. Engels ([1878] 1947):417-18.

22. Ibid., 339.

23. Ibid., 343-44. See also Engels ([1895a] 1982):455.

24. Marx ([1867] 1967):80.

25. Marx ([1894] 1967):820.

26. Engels ([1878] 1947):408-09; ([1895b] 1982):459.

27. Marx ([1894] 1967):820.

28. Marx ([1857-58] 1973):694, 706.

29. Marx ([1863a] 1963):391, 307.

30. Marx ([1857-58] 1973):161.

31. Ibid.

32. Marx ([1894] 1967):189.

33. Avineri (1968):68.

34. Althusser (1971):133.

35. On the calculation debate, see Hayek ([1933] 1975); Mises ([1920] 1933); ([1936] 1951); and especially Lavoie (1981); (1985b); (1985c). Lavoie (1985c) offers the most provocative reconsideration of the debate. It is a fascinating intellectual exchange in the history of economic thought. Lavoie expands on Misesian and Hayekian insights as he integrates Austrian theory with elements of hermeneutics. See also, his critique of all forms of *National Economic Planning* (1985b).

36. Wainwright (1994):50.

37. Many other economists absorbed Austrian insights, including Gottfried Haberler, Fritz Machlup, Oskar Morgenstern, and Joseph Schumpeter. The contemporary Austrian school includes Peter Boettke, Richard Ebeling, Roger Garrison, Israel Kirzner, (the late) Ludwig Lachmann, Don Lavoie, Stephen Littlechild, Gerald O'Driscoll, Mario Rizzo, (the late) Murray Rothbard, George Selgin, and Lawrence White, among others.

38. While I have explored some of the common German and Scottish philosophical roots of Marxian and Hayekian dialectics, I have not examined to any great extent, their common Aristotelian roots. While Marx's method is indebted to Aristotelian philosophy (see Chapter Five), the modern Austrian school has combined Aristotelian and Kantian influences. Hayek's mentor, Ludwig von Mises, was a philosophical Kantian. But the older Austrian school was more firmly entrenched in Aristotelian realism. Menger and Boehm-Bawerk have been characterized as Aristotelians. Emil Kauder argues that the Aristotelian influence on Menger's method "can be well docu-

mented." See Kauder (1957), "Intellectual and Political Roots of the Older Austrian School," in Littlechild (1990):12. Menger's characteristically dynamic approach sounds profoundly Hegelian at times, especially in its emphasis on the process of "becoming." See for instance, Menger ([1871] 1950):67. Menger studied Aristotle's metaphysics and epistemology intensely prior to writing his methodological expositions. This Aristotelian legacy was passed on to future generations of Austrian school theorists, including to some extent, Hayek. A full documentation of these intellectual influences is beyond the scope of the current study.

39. Both Marx and Hayek share the view that the economic sphere cannot be abstracted from culture, law, politics, and the like, since each is a constituent part of an organic totality. Kukathas notes correctly that this perspective is rooted in the thought of Hegel. See Kukathas (1989):56. He writes:

> Like Hegel, [Hayek] sees the economy or, as he prefers to call it, the "catallaxy", not as a separate realm to be understood abstracted from the processes of social life but as intelligible only within the system of rule-governed relationships among individuals in the extended order of society.

40. On the "transformation problem" see Sweezy ([1949] 1975) which includes original essays by Boehm-Bawerk ([1896] 1949) and Hilferding ([1904] 1949). Also see Meek ([1956] 1976). Sowell, himself influenced by both the Chicago and Austrian schools, maintains that Boehm-Bawerk mistook Marx's labor theory of value for a theory of individual commodity prices. Sowell [(1985):89] argues that Marx "flatly contradicted this. . . . The law of value was thus essentially a principle of resource allocation, rather than of price determination."

41. Mises ([1920] 1933):111.

42. See Lippincott (1964) for a summary of the "market socialist" perspective of Oskar Lange and Fred M. Taylor.

43. Hayek (1988):14, 19.

44. Ibid., 77.

45. Ibid., 84.

46. Ibid., 95.

47. Lavoie (1985b):6.

48. Hayek (1988):80.

49. Lavoie (1985b):58.

50. On the Austrian concept of entrepreneurship see Kirzner (1973); (1984*a*); (1984*b*).

51. Lavoie (1985*b*):66.

52. Hayek (1988):9.

53. Heilbroner (1990):92. On Soviet history and political economy, see Nove (1969); (1978); (1980); (1983); and especially, Boettke (1990); (1993). As an indication of the changes in Communist ideology that accompanied this movement away from central planning, see Gorbachev (1988).

54. Hayek (1944):xii.

55. Ibid., vii.

56. Wainwright (1994):7.

57. Hayek ([1970] 1978):20.

58. Hayek (1976):25.

59. For a brief discussion of "statist dualism," see Chapter One.

60. Marx ([1871] 1968):289, 292.

61. Hayek (1981):173, 176.

62. Hayek (1976):30.

63. Ibid., 39.

64. Like Hayek, Merleau-Ponty argues that there is no human choice that can terminate unexpected consequences or that can exhaust man's creative power leading to an end to history. See Merleau-Ponty (1973):23.

65. In this regard, I will discuss some of Wainwright's proposals in Chapter Seven.

66. Engels ([1875] 1982):275-76.

67. Hayek ([1946] 1948):15.

68. Wartofsky (1983):16.

Chapter 7

1. Trotsky ([1924] 1960):255-56.

2. Wainwright (1994):96.

3. Of course, Hunt [(1984):xi] argues that the notion of "participatory democracy" lies at "the core of Marx and Engels' political ideas." See Hunt (1974); (1984). A discussion of this issue is beyond the scope of the current study.

4. Kellner (1989):1.

5. Marcuse (1972):55.

6. Habermas (1987b):329.

7. McCarthy in Habermas ([1976] 1979):viii.

8. Tar (1977):113-14; Piccone (1973):18-19.

9. Adorno ([1966] 1983):406.

10. Adorno advances a theory of "negative dialectic" that refuses to grant primacy to either pole of any duality. According to Adorno, difference is not a quality between two things; it is characteristic of the thing itself. This principle allegedly negates the law of identity. Despite his nihilistic quest to invalidate all of metaphysics, epistemology, and dualistic method, Adorno draws attention to "contradiction" as an illuminating ontological category. Adorno's works are extremely intricate and complex, and I generally agree with Kolakowski's view that they are also hopelessly pessimistic. See Kolakowski (1984):114.

11. Here, the phrase "new left" does not refer to the New Left movement of the 1960s. It is a phrase adopted from Wainwright (1994), a book which critiques Hayek's theory of knowledge in an attempt to reconstitute the Left.

12. Habermas ([1976] 1979):95.

13. Wainwright (1994):92.

14. McCarthy in Habermas ([1976] 1979):ix-x.

15. Habermas ([1971] 1973):1-2.

16. Habermas ([1976] 1979):98.

17. Ibid., 118.

18. Habermas ([1967] 1988):xiv.

19. See Habermas (1975); (1976a); (1976b). Also see McCarthy (1978):86, 133. McCarthy's work provides a clear and concise introduction to Habermas's thought.

20. Habermas ([1971] 1973):17.

21. Habermas (1970):372.

22. Habermas ([1976] 1979):3-5.

23. Ibid., 2-3.

24. Ibid., 29, 63. See also McCarthy (1978):276-77.

25. Habermas ([1976] 1979):63.

26. Ibid., 15.

27. Polanyi ([1958] 1962):206.

28. Ibid., 250.

29. Habermas, "A reply to my critics," in Thompson and Held (1982):264.

30. Habermas ([1971] 1973):9.

31. Habermas ([1968] 1971):217.

32. Ibid., 218-19.

33. Ibid., 220-21.

34. Ibid., 229.

35. Ibid., 230.

36. Ibid., 233, 235-36.

37. See Habermas (1987*a*) and Dews (1992), in which Habermas seems much more sympathetic to spontaneous order arguments concerning the acquisition and dissemination of knowledge.

38. Habermas (1994):26.

39. Hayek (1988):134. See also Kukathas (1989):61; Livingston (1991):164.

40. Hayek (1988):64.

41. Wainwright (1994):92-93.

42. Ibid., xi.

43. Ibid., 45.

44. Ibid., xii.

45. Ibid., xiii-xiv.

46. Ibid., 1.

47. See Wootton (1945); Crosland (1957).

48. Ibid., 5.

49. Ibid., 54, 270. I do not address Hayek's constitutional proposals in this work. While Wainwright is correct to criticize aspects of Hayek's proposed changes, she fails to consider any works beyond *The Constitution of Liberty*. See ibid., 53. As for monopolies and externalities, Wainwright does not consider the vast libertarian literature that roots such phenomena in political, rather than purely market, factors. In this regard, Wainwright accepts the standard Marxist arguments. For instance, Engels [([1844] 1964):223] names apothecaries and the money supply as two articles requiring a government monopoly. Several economists have argued, however, that the market can provide—and has provided—for "public" goods. They suggest that externalities can be "internalized" through legal and institutional modifications. Their writings have figured prominently in the debate over privatization. On the whole phenomenon of public goods, see Rothbard ([1956] 1977); Coase (1974); Manne (1975); Fielding (1979); Block (1979); (1983); Brownstein (1980); Cowen (1985); (1988). Hayek [(1988):36] cites Coase and Demsetz, among others, as significant theorists who have investigated expansive property rights definitions in the legal framework of the market. Some Marxists, such as Poulantzas, have also recognized the role that the provision of public goods has played in the growth of state power. See Poulantzas (1978):37. On the role of the state in creating monopolies, see Mises ([1949] 1963); Rothbard ([1970] 1977); (1978b).

50. Wainwright (1994):5, 28, 268.

51. Ibid., 57.

52. Hayek ([1946] 1948):14.

53. Wainwright (1994):58, 169.

54. Ibid., 58.

55. Ibid., 13.

56. Ibid., 91-93.

57. Ibid., 58-61.

58. Ibid., 80-81.

59. Ibid., 83.

60. Ibid.

61. Ibid., 106.

62. Ibid., 107.

63. Ibid., 108, 118.

64. Ibid., 140.

65. Ibid., 190, 265.

66. Ibid., 272, 283.

67. Ibid., 141.

68. Ibid., 148. Wainwright [(1994):182-84] discusses too, the contributions of Prychitko (1991), who combines elements of Marxian and Hayekian analysis in his examination of "the essential tension" between Marxism and "worker self-management."

69. Ibid., 197.

70. Hayek (1973):36.

Epilogue

1. Marx ([1843] 1963):52.

2. Hayek ([1976] 1978):296.

3. Hayek (1988):22.

4. Hayek (1960):114.

5. Hayek (1973):64-65.

6. Kukathas (1989):211. See also Steele [(1992):375] who argues that no one can escape from "utopianism," that is, from the need to construct social ideals. For Steele, as for Hayek, it is a legitimate task of social science to "criticize our utopias, discard those convicted of unfeasibility, and replace them with better utopias."

7. Hayek ([1949] 1967):194.

8. Boettke [(1988):34, 50, n.34] recognizes my own "alternative Hayekian discussion" as a movement toward a non-Marxist, anti-utopian, "critical theory," which integrates libertarian values and Hayekian strictures. In the development of this project, see Sciabarra (1995), which is a provocative sequel to the current work. It presents Ayn Rand as among the foremost libertarian contributors to a non-Marxist, dialectical, radical social science.

References

Acton, H. B. [1955] 1973. *The Illusion of the Epoch: Marxism-Leninism as a Philosophical Creed*. London: Routledge and Kegan-Paul.

Adorno, Theodor W. [1966] 1983. *Negative Dialectics*. Translated by E. B. Ashton. New York: Continuum.

Alexander, Jeffrey C. 1982*a*. *Theoretical Logic in Sociology, Volume One: Positivism, Presuppositions, and Current Controversies*. Berkeley: University of California.

———. 1982*b*. *Theoretical Logic in Sociology, Volume Two: The Antinomies of Classical Thought: Marx and Durkheim*. Berkeley: University of California Press.

Althusser, Louis. 1971. *Lenin and Philosophy and Other Essays*. Translated from the French by Ben Brewster. London: NLB.

Althusser, Louis and E. Balibar. [1970] 1971. *Reading "Capital."* London: New Left; New York: Pantheon.

Antonio, Robert J. 1987. "Reason and History in Hayek." *Critical Review* 1, no. 2 (Spring):58-73.

Aristotle. 1941. *The Basic Works of Aristotle*. Edited, with introduction by Richard McKeon. New York: Random House.

Avineri, Shlomo. 1968. *The Social and Political Thought of Karl Marx*. Cambridge, England: Cambridge University Press.

———. 1980. *Hegel's Theory of the Modern State*. Cambridge, England: Cambridge University Press.

Barber, Benjamin R. 1986. "Where We Learn Democracy." Review of *Free Spaces: The Sources of Democratic Change in America*, by Sara M. Evans and Harry C. Boyle. *The New York Times Book Review*, 9 March:15.

Barry, Norman. 1979. *Hayek's Social and Economic Philosophy*. London: Macmillan.

——. 1982. "The Tradition of Spontaneous Order." *Literature of Liberty* 5, no. 2 (Summer):7-58.

——. 1983. Review article: "The New Liberalism." *British Journal of Political Science* 13, pt. 1 (January):99-123.

Bartley, W. W., III. 1984. "Knowledge Is a Product Not Fully Known to Its Producer." In Leube and Zlabinger 1984: pp. 17-45.

——. 1990. *Unfathomed Knowledge, Unmeasured Wealth*. LaSalle, Ill.: Open Court.

Bernstein, Richard J. 1971. *Praxis and Action: Contemporary Philosophies of Human Activity*. Philadelphia: University of Pennsylvania Press.

——. [1976] 1978. *The Restructuring of Social and Political Theory*. Philadelphia: University of Pennsylvania Press; Harcourt Brace Jovanovich.

——. 1983. *Beyond Objectivism and Relativism: Science, Hermeneutics, and Praxis*. Philadelphia: University of Pennsylvania Press.

Bettelheim, Charles. 1975. *The Transition to Socialist Economy*. Translated from the French by Brian Pearce. Atlantic Highlands, N.J.: Humanities.

Blackburn, Robin, ed. 1972. *Ideology in Social Science: Readings in Critical Theory*. New York: Pantheon.

Blanshard, Brand. 1940. *The Nature of Thought*. 2 vols. New York: Macmillan.

——. 1962. *Reason and Analysis*. LaSalle, Ill.: Open Court.

Block, Walter. 1979. "Free Market Transportation: Denationalizing the Roads." *The Journal of Libertarian Studies* 3, no. 2 (Summer):209-38.

——. 1983. "Public Goods and Externalities: The Case of Roads." *The Journal of Libertarian Studies* 7, no. 1 (Spring):1-34.

Bobbio, Noberto. 1979. "Gramsci and the Conception of Civil Society." In Mouffe 1979.

Boehm-Bawerk, Eugen von. [1896] 1949. "Karl Marx and the Close of His System." In Sweezy [1949] 1975.

Boettke, Peter J. 1988. "Economists and Liberty: Murray N. Rothbard." *Nomos* 6, nos. 3-4 (Fall/Winter).

——. 1990. *The Political Economy of Soviet Socialism: The Formative Years, 1918-1928*. Boston: Kluwer.

——. 1993. *Why Perestroika Failed: The Politics and Economics of Socialist Transformation*. London and New York: Routledge.

Bottomore, Tom, ed. 1983. *A Dictionary of Marxist Thought*. Cambridge, Mass.: Harvard University Press.

Branden, Nathaniel. 1969. *The Psychology of Self-Esteem: A New Concept of Man's Psychological Nature*. Los Angeles: Nash.

———. [1969] 1974. "Free Will, Moral Responsibility, and the Law." In Machan 1974, pp. 419-44.

———. 1971. *The Disowned Self*. Los Angeles: Nash.

———. 1983. *Honoring the Self: Personal Integrity and the Heroic Potentials of Human Nature*. Los Angeles: Jeremy P. Tarcher.

Brien, Kevin M. 1987. *Marx, Reason, and the Art of Freedom*. Philadelphia: Temple University Press.

Brownstein, Barry P. 1980. "Pareto Optimality, External Benefits and Public Goods: A Subjectivist Approach." *The Journal of Libertarian Studies* 4, no. 1 (Winter):93-106.

Bullock, Alan. 1962. *Hitler: A Study in Tyranny*. New York: Harper and Row.

Burke, Edmund. [1790] 1955. *Reflections on the Revolution in France*. Reprint edited by Thomas H. D. Mahoney. Indianapolis: Bobbs-Merrill.

Butler, Eamonn. 1983. *Hayek: His Contribution to the Political and Economic Thought of Our Time*. New York: Universe.

Caputo, John D. 1988. "Presidential Address: Radical Hermeneutics and the Human Condition." In *Hermeneutics and the Tradition*. Vol. 62 Proceedings. Edited by Daniel O. Dahlstrom. Washington, D.C.: National Office of the American Catholic Philosophical Association.

Childs, R. A., Jr. 1974. "Liberty and the Paradigm of Statism." In Machan 1974: pp. 502-24.

Coase, Ronald. 1974. "The lighthouse in economics." *The Journal of Law and Economics* 17:357-76.

Cohen, G. A. 1978. *Karl Marx's Theory of History: A Defence*. Princeton: Princeton University Press.

Copleston, Frederick, S. J. [1946] 1985. *A History of Philosophy, Volume I: Greece and Rome*. Garden City, N.Y.: Image.

———. 1985. *A History of Philosophy, Book Three, Volume 7: Fichte to Nietzsche*. Garden City, N.Y.: Doubleday, Image.

Cowen, Tyler. 1985. "A Public Goods Definition and Their Institutional Context: A Critique of Public Goods Theory." *Review of Social Economy* 63, no. 1 (April):53-63.

————, ed. 1988. *The Theory of Market Failure: A Critical Examination.* Fairfax, Va.: George Mason University Press.

Crosland, Charles Anthony Raven. 1957. *The Future of Socialism.* New York: Macmillan.

Dews, Peter, ed. 1992. *Autonomy and Solidarity: Interviews with Jürgen Habermas,* rev. ed. New York: Verso.

Diamond, Arthur M., Jr. 1980. "F. A. Hayek on Constructivism and Ethics." *The Journal of Libertarian Studies* 4, no. 4 (Fall):353-65.

Draper, Hal. 1977. *Karl Marx's Theory of Revolution, Volume 1: State and Bureaucracy.* New York: Monthly Review.

East, John P. 1980. "The American Conservative Movement of the 1980s: Are Traditional and Libertarian Dimensions Compatible?" *Modern Age* 24, no. 1 (Winter):34-38.

Ebeling, Richard M. 1985. "Hermeneutics and the Interpretive Element in the Analysis of the Market Process." *Center for the Study of Market Processes Working Paper Series* 16. Department of Economics, George Mason University.

Elster, Jon. 1983. *Explaining Technical Change: A Case Study in the Philosophy of Science.* Cambridge, England: Cambridge University Press.

————. 1985. *Making Sense of Marx.* Cambridge, England: Cambridge University Press.

————. 1986. *An Introduction to Karl Marx.* Cambridge, England: Cambridge University Press.

Engels, Frederick. [1844] 1964. "Outlines of a Critique of Political Economy." In Karl Marx [1844] 1964.

————. [1871] 1968. "Apropos of Working-Class Political Action." In Marx and Engels 1968.

————. [1875] 1982. Letter to August Bebel (18-28 March). In Marx and Engels 1982.

————. [1878] 1947. *Herr Eugen Dühring's Revolution in Science.* Moscow: Progress.

————. [1880] 1968. *Socialism: Utopian and Scientific.* In Marx and Engels 1968.

————. [1881a] 1982. Letter to Karl Kautsky (1 February). In Marx and Engels 1968.

———. [1881*b*] 1982. Letter to Eduard Bernstein (12 March). In Marx and Engels 1982.

———. [1883] 1982. Letter to Phil van Patten (18 April). In Marx and Engels 1982.

———. [1884] 1968. *The Origin of the Family, Private Property and the State*. In Marx and Engels 1968.

———. [1885] 1982. Letter to V. I. Zasulich (23 April). In Marx and Engels 1982.

———. [1886] 1968. *Ludwig Feuerbach and the End of Classical German Philosophy*. In Marx and Engels 1968.

———. [1890*a*] 1982. Letter to Conrad Schmidt (5 August). In Marx and Engels 1982.

———. [1890*b*] 1982. Letter to Joseph Bloch (21-22 September). In Marx and Engels 1982.

———. [1890*c*] 1982. Letter to Conrad Schmidt (27 October). In Marx and Engels 1982.

———. [1891] 1968. Introduction to *The Civil War in France* by Karl Marx. In Marx and Engels 1968.

———. [1893] 1982. Letter to N. F. Danielson (17 October). In Marx and Engels 1982.

———. [1894] 1968. *The Peasant Question in France and Germany*. In Marx and Engels 1968.

———. [1894] 1982. Letter to W. Borgius (25 January). In Marx and Engels 1982.

———. [1895*a*] 1982. Letter to Werner Sombart (11 March). In Marx and Engels 1982.

———. [1895*b*] 1982. Letter to Conrad Schmidt (12 March). In Marx and Engels 1982.

Fichte, Johann Gottlieb. [1794] 1970. *The Science of Knowledge*. Edited, translated by Peter Heath and John Lachs. New York: Appleton-Century-Crofts.

Fielding, Karl T. 1979. "Nonexcludability and Government Financing of Public Goods." *The Journal of Libertarian Studies* 3, no. 3 (Fall):293-98.

Flacks, Richard. 1982. "Marxism and Sociology." In Ollman and Vernoff 1982: pp. 9-52.

Friedman, Jeffrey. 1991. "Postmodernism versus Postlibertarianism." *Critical Review* 5, no. 2 (Spring):145-58.

Friedman, Milton. 1962. *Capitalism and Freedom*. Chicago: University of Chicago Press.

Gadamer, Hans-Georg. 1982. *Truth and Method*. New York: Crossroads.

Geddes, John M. 1979. "New Vogue for Critic of Keynes." *The New York Times* (7 May):D1, D7.

Gerth, H. H. and C. Wright Mills, eds. 1946. *From Max Weber: Essays in Sociology*. New York: Oxford University Press.

Giddens, Anthony. 1979. *Central Problems in Social Theory: Action, Structure and Contradiction in Social Analysis*. Berkeley: University of California Press.

Godelier, Maurice. 1972. "Structure and Contradiction in *Capital*." In Blackburn 1972: pp. 334-68.

Gorbachev, Mikhail. 1988. *Perestroika: New Thinking for Our Country and the World*, new, rev. ed. New York: Harper and Row.

Gotthelf, Allan. 1976. "Aristotle's Conception of Final Causality." In Gotthelf and Lennox 1987.

Gotthelf, Allan and James G. Lennox, eds. 1987. *Philosophical Issues in Aristotle's Biology*. New York: Cambridge University Press.

Gould, Carol C. 1978. *Marx's Social Ontology: Individuality and Community in Marx's Theory of Social Reality*. Cambridge, Mass.: MIT Press.

Gramsci, Antonio. 1971. *Selections from the Prison Notebooks of Antonio Gramsci*. Edited, translated by Quentin Hoare and Geoffrey Nowell Smith. New York: International.

Gray, John. 1980. "F. A. Hayek on Liberty and Tradition." *The Journal of Libertarian Studies* 4, no. 2 (Spring):119-34.

———. 1982. "F. A. Hayek and the Rebirth of Classical Liberalism." *Literature of Liberty* 5, no. 4 (Winter):19-101.

———. 1984. *Hayek on Liberty*. New York: Basil Blackwell.

Guerin, Daniel. [1939] 1973. *Fascism and Big Business*. Translated by Frances and Mason Merrill. New York: Monad, Pathfinder.

Habermas, Jürgen. [1967] 1988. *On the Logic of the Social Sciences*. Translated by Shierry Weber Nicholsen and Jerry A. Stark; introduction by Thomas McCarthy. Cambridge, Mass.: MIT Press.

———. [1968] 1971. *Knowledge and Human Interests*. Translated by Jeremy J. Shapiro. Boston: Beacon.

———. 1970. "Toward a Theory of Communicative Competence." *Inquiry* 13.

———. [1971] 1973. *Theory and Practice*. Boston: Beacon.

———. 1975. *Legitimation Crisis*. Translated by Thomas McCarthy. Boston: Beacon.

———. 1976a. "The Analytical Theory of Science and Dialectics." In *The Positivist Dispute in German Sociology*, translated by Glyn Adey and David Frisby, pp. 131-62. London: Heinemann Educational.

———. 1976b. "A Positivistically Bisected Rationalism." In *The Positivist Dispute in German Sociology*, translated by Glyn Adey and David Frisby, pp. 198-225. London: Heinemann Educational.

———. [1976] 1979. *Communication and the Evolution of Society*. Translated, introduction by Thomas McCarthy. Boston: Beacon.

———. 1987a. *The Theory of Communicative Action—Volume 1: Reason and the Rationalization of Society*. Boston: Beacon.

———. 1987b. *The Theory of Communicative Action—Volume 2: Lifeworld and System: A Critique of Functionalist Reason*. Boston: Beacon.

———. 1994. "'More Humility, Fewer Illusions'—A Talk between Adam Michnik and Jürgen Habermas." *The New York Review of Books* XLI, no. 6 (24 March):24-29.

Hacking, Ian, ed. 1981. *Scientific Revolutions*. Oxford Readings in Philosophy. Oxford: Oxford University Press.

Hart, David M. 1981-82. "Gustave de Molinari and the Anti-statist Liberal Tradition." Parts 1-3. *Journal of Libertarian Studies* 5, no. 3:263-90; 5, no. 4:399-434; 6, no. 1:83-104.

Hartz, Louis. 1955. *The Liberal Tradition in America*. New York: Harcourt, Brace and World.

Hayek, F. A. [1929] 1966. *Monetary Theory and the Trade Cycle*. New York: Augustus M. Kelley.

———. [1931] 1967. *Prices and Production*. New York: Augustus M. Kelley.

———, ed. [1933] 1975. *Collectivist Economic Planning*. Clifton: Augustus M. Kelley.

———. [1933] 1991. "The Trend of Economic Thinking." In Hayek 1991.

——— . [1937] 1948. "Economics and Knowledge." In Hayek 1948.

——— . [1943] 1948. "The Facts of the Social Sciences." In Hayek 1948.

——— . 1944. *The Road to Serfdom*. Chicago: University of Chicago Press.

——— . [1945] 1948. "The Use of Knowledge in Society." In Hayek 1948.

——— . [1946] 1948. "Individualism: True and False." In Hayek 1948.

——— . 1948. *Individualism and Economic Order*. Chicago: University of Chicago Press.

——— . [1949] 1967. "The Intellectuals and Socialism." In Hayek [1967] 1980.

——— . [1952] 1976. *The Sensory Order: An Inquiry into the Foundations of Theoretical Psychology*. Chicago: University of Chicago Press, Midway Reprints.

——— , ed. 1954. *Capitalism and the Historians*. London: Routledge and Kegan Paul and Chicago: University of Chicago Press.

——— . [1955] 1967. "Degrees of Explanation." In Hayek [1967] 1980.

——— . [1956a] 1967. "The Dilemma of Specialization." In Hayek [1967] 1980.

——— . [1956b] 1967. "*The Road to Serfdom* after Twelve Years." In Hayek [1967] 1980.

——— . [1957] 1967. "What Is 'Social'? What Does It Mean?" In Hayek [1967] 1980.

——— . 1960. *The Constitution of Liberty*. Chicago: University of Chicago Press.

——— . 1961. "Freedom and Coercion: Some Comments and Mr. Hamowy's Criticism." *New Individualist Review* 1, no. 2 (Summer):28-29.

——— . [1962a] 1967. "The Moral Element in Free Enterprise." In Hayek [1967] 1980.

——— . [1962b] 1967. "Rules, Perception and Intelligibility." In Hayek [1967] 1980.

——— . [1964] 1967. "The Theory of Complex Phenomena." In Hayek [1967] 1980.

——— . [1965] 1967. "Kinds of Rationalism." In Hayek [1967] 1980.

——— . [1966] 1967. "The Principles of a Liberal Social Order." In Hayek [1967] 1980.

————. [1966] 1991. "Dr. Bernard Mandeville: 1670-1733." In Hayek 1991.

————. 1967. "Notes on the Evolution of Systems of Rules of Conduct." In Hayek [1967] 1980.

————. [1967] 1980. *Studies in Philosophy, Politics, and Economics.* Chicago: University of Chicago Press, Midway Reprints.

————. [1968*a*] 1978. "The Confusion of Language in Political Thought." In Hayek [1978] 1985.

————. [1968*b*] 1978. "Competition as a Discovery Procedure." In Hayek [1978] 1985.

————. [1970] 1978. "The Errors of Constructivism." In Hayek [1978] 1985.

————. 1973. *Law, Legislation and Liberty, Volume 1: Rules and Order.* Chicago: University of Chicago Press.

————. 1976. *Law, Legislation and Liberty, Volume 2: The Mirage of Social Justice.* Chicago: University of Chicago Press.

————. [1976] 1978. "Socialism and Science." In Hayek [1978] 1985.

————. 1978. *The Denationalization of Money,* 2d ed. London: Institute of Economic Affairs.

————. [1978] 1985. *New Studies in Philosophy, Politics, Economics, and the History of Ideas.* Chicago: University of Chicago Press.

————. 1981. *Law, Legislation and Liberty, Volume 3: The Political Order of a Free People.* Chicago: University of Chicago Press.

————. 1984. *The Essence of Hayek.* Edited by Chiaki Nishiyama and Kurt R. Leube; foreword by W. Glenn Campbell. Stanford, Calif.: Hoover Institution.

————. 1988. *The Fatal Conceit: The Errors of Socialism—Volume I: The Collected Works of F. A. Hayek.* Edited by W. W. Bartley III. Chicago: University of Chicago Press.

————. 1991. *The Trend of Economic Thinking: Essays on Political Economists and Economic History—Volume III: The Collected Works of F. A. Hayek.* Edited by W. W. Bartley III and Stephen Kresge. Chicago: University of Chicago Press.

————. 1992. *The Fortunes of Liberalism: Essays on Austrian Economics and the Ideal of Freedom—Volume IV: The Collected Works of F. A. Hayek.* Edited by Peter G. Klein. Chicago: University of Chicago Press.

Hegel, G. W. F. [1807] 1977. *Phenomenology of Spirit.* Translated by A. V. Miller; analysis, foreword by J. N. Findlay. Oxford: Oxford University Press.

————. [1812-16] 1969. *The Science of Logic*, 2 vols. Translated by A. V. Miller. London: George Allen & Unwin.

Heilbroner, Robert. 1981. *Marxism: For and Against*. New York: W. W. Norton.

————. 1987. "The Dialectical Approach to Philosophy." In Machan 1987: pp. 2-18.

————. 1990. "Reflections: After Communism." *The New Yorker* (10 September):91-100.

Hellman, Geoffrey. 1979. "Historical Materialism." In Mepham and Ruben 1979.

Heydebrand, Wolf. 1980. Review symposium. Review of *The System of Modern Societies* by Talcott Parsons. *Contemporary Sociology: A Journal of Reviews* (June):387-95.

————. 1981. "Marxist Structuralism." In *Continuities in Structural Inquiry*, edited by Peter Blau and Robert Merton, pp. 81-119. London: Sage.

————. 1983. "Organization and Praxis." In *Beyond Method: Strategies for Social Research*, edited by Gareth Morgan, pp. 306-20. Beverly Hills, Calif.: Sage.

Heydebrand, Wolf and Beverly Burris. 1982. "The Limits of Praxis in Critical Theory." In *The Frankfurt School Revisited*, edited by Judith Marcus and Zoltan Tar. New York: Columbia University Press.

Hilferding, Rudolph. [1904] 1949. "Boehm-Bawerk's Criticism of Marx." In Sweezy [1949] 1975.

Hook, Sidney. [1936] 1950. *From Hegel to Marx: Studies in the Intellectual Development of Karl Marx*. New York: Reynal and Hitchcock.

Hunt, R. N. Carew. 1950. *The Theory and Practice of Communism: An Introduction*. London: Geoffrey Bles.

Hunt, Richard N. 1974. *The Political Ideas of Marx and Engels, Vol. 1: Marxism and Totalitarian Democracy, 1818-1850*. Pittsburgh: University of Pittsburgh Press.

————. 1984. *The Political Ideas of Marx and Engels, Vol. 2: Classical Marxism*. Pittsburgh: University of Pittsburgh Press.

Irwin, Terence. 1988. *Aristotle's First Principles*. New York: Oxford University Press; Oxford: Clarendon.

Jay, Martin. 1973. *The Dialectical Imagination: A History of the Frankfurt School and the Institute of Social Research, 1923-1950*. Boston: Little, Brown.

Kauder, Emil. 1957. "Intellectual and Political Roots of the Older Austrian School." In Littlechild 1990.

Kelley, David. 1986. *The Evidence of the Senses: A Realist Theory of Perception*. Baton Rouge: Louisiana State University Press.

Kelley, David, moderator. 1993. "Colloquium on Chris Sciabarra's *Ayn Rand: The Russian Radical*." Sponsored by the Institute for Objectivist Studies, New York City. (6 June).

Kellner, Douglas. 1989. *Critical Theory, Marxism, and Modernity*. Baltimore: Johns Hopkins University Press.

Kirk, Russell. [1953] 1986. *The Conservative Mind: From Burke to Eliot*, 7th rev. ed. Chicago: Henry Regnery.

Kirzner, Israel M. 1973. *Competition and Entrepreneurship*. Chicago: University of Chicago Press.

——— . 1984*a*. "Economic Planning and the Knowledge Problem." *Cato Journal* 4, no. 2 (Fall):407-25.

——— . 1984*b*. "Prices, the Communication of Knowledge and the Discovery Process." In Leube and Zlabinger 1984: pp. 193-206.

——— . 1992. *The Meaning of the Market Process: Essays in the Development of Modern Austrian Economics*. London and New York: Routledge.

Kolakowski, Leszek. 1978. *Main Currents of Marxism: Its Origins, Growth and Dissolution, Vol. 1: The Founders*. Translated by P. S. Falla. New York: Oxford University Press.

——— . 1984. "The Frankfurt School and Critical Theory." In Marcus and Tar 1984: pp. 95-116.

Kolko, Gabriel. 1963. *The Triumph of Conservatism: A Reinterpretation of American History, 1900-1916*. New York: Free Press.

Kuhn, Thomas. 1970. *The Structure of Scientific Revolutions*, 2d ed., enlarged. Chicago: University of Chicago Press.

Kukathas, Chandron. 1989. *Hayek and Modern Liberalism*. Oxford: Clarendon.

Lakatos, Imre and Alan Musgrave. 1970. *Criticism and the Growth of Knowledge*. New York: Cambridge University Press.

Lavoie, Don, ed. 1981. "An Economic Critique of Socialism." *The Journal of Libertarian Studies* 5, no. 1 (Winter).

——— . 1982. "The Market as a Procedure for the Discovery and Convergence of Inarticulate Knowledge." *Center for the Study of Market Processes: Working Paper Series* 100-2, Department of Economics, George Mason University (November).

——— . 1985*a*. "The Interpretive Dimension of Economics: Science, Hermeneutics, and Praxeology." *Center for the Study of Market Processes: Working Paper Series* 15, Department of Economics, George Mason University.

——— . 1985*b*. *National Economic Planning: What Is Left?* Cambridge, Mass.: Ballinger.

——— . 1985*c*. *Rivalry and Central Planning: The Socialist Calculation Debate Reconsidered.* New York: Cambridge University Press.

——— , ed. 1991. *Economics and Hermeneutics.* New York: Routledge.

Lefebvre, Henri. 1968*a*. *Dialectical Materialism.* Translated from the French by John Sturrock. London: Jonathan Cape.

——— . 1968*b*. *The Sociology of Marx.* Translated from the French by Norbert Guterman. New York: Pantheon.

Lemieux, Pierre. 1994. "Exploration: Chaos, Complexity, and Anarchy." *Liberty* 7 (March):21-29, 52.

Lenin, V. I. [1908] 1939. *Selected Works—The Theoretical Principles of Marxism.* Vol. 11. New York: International.

——— . [1914-16] 1963. On Aristotle's *Metaphysics.* In Selsam and Martel 1963.

Leube, Kurt R., and Albert H. Zlabinger, eds. 1984. *The Political Economy of Freedom: Essays in Honor of F. A. Hayek.* Munchen Wien: Philosophia Verlag.

Lichtheim, George. [1964] 1982. *Marxism: An Historical and Critical Study.* New York: Columbia University Press.

Lippincott, Benjamin E., ed. 1964. *On the Economic Theory of Socialism.* New York: McGraw-Hill.

Littlechild, Stephen, ed. 1990. *Austrian Economics: Volume I.* Schools of Thought in Economics. Series Editor: Mark Blaug. England and Brookfield, Vt.: Edward Elgar.

Livingston, Donald W. 1991. "Hayek as Humean." *Critical Review* 5, no. 2 (Spring):159-77.

Lowi, Theodore. [1969] 1979. *The End of Liberalism*, 2d ed. New York: W. W. Norton.

Lúkacs, Georg. [1919] 1971. "What Is Orthodox Marxism?" In Lúkacs 1971:1-26.

———. 1971. *History and Class Consciousness: Studies in Marxist Dialectics*. Translated by Rodney Livingstone. Cambridge, Mass.: MIT Press.

Lukes, Steven. 1968. "Methodological Individualism Reconsidered." *British Journal of Sociology* 19:119-29.

Machan, Tibor R., ed. 1974. *The Libertarian Alternative*. Chicago: Nelson-Hall.

———, ed. 1987. *The Main Debate: Communism versus Capitalism*. New York: Random House.

———. 1988. Reply to Chris Sciabarra. *Critical Review* 2 (Spring):226-27.

MacIntyre, Alasdair. [1971] 1973. "The Idea of a Social Science." In Ryan 1973: pp. 15-32.

Madison, G. B. 1990. "How Individualistic is Methodological Individualism?" *Critical Review* 4, nos. 1-2 (Winter-Spring):41-60.

Manne, Henry G., ed. 1975. *The Economics of Legal Relationships*. New York: West.

Marcus, Judith and Zoltan Tar, eds. 1984. *Foundations of the Frankfurt School of Social Research*. New Brunswick: Transaction.

Marcuse, Herbert. [1941] 1960. *Reason and Revolution: Hegel and the Rise of Social Theory*. Boston: Beacon.

———. 1972. *Studies in Critical Philosophy*. Translated by Joris de Bres. London: NLB.

Marx, Karl. [1842] 1967. "On a Proposed Divorce Law." In Marx 1967.

———. [1843] 1963. "The Critique of Hegel's Philosophy of Right." In Marx 1963.

———. [1843-44] 1967. "On the Jewish Question." In Marx 1967.

———. [1844] 1964. *Economic and Philosophic Manuscripts of 1844*. Edited, introduction by Dirk J. Struik; translated by Martin Mulligan. New York: International.

———. [1844a] 1967. Critical notes on "The King of Prussia and Social Reform." In Marx 1967.

———. [1844*b*] 1967. Excerpt-notes of 1844. In Marx 1967.

———. [1845] 1967. Theses on Feuerbach. In Marx 1967.

———. [1846] 1982. Letter to P. V. Annenkov (28 December). In Marx and Engels 1982.

———. [1847] 1967. "The Poverty of Philosophy." In Marx 1967.

———. [1847] 1976. "Wage-labour and Capital." In Marx 1976.

———. [1852] 1963. *The Eighteenth Brumaire of Louis Bonaparte.* New York: International.

———. [1857-58] 1973. *Grundrisse: Introduction to the Critique of Political Economy.* Translated, foreword by Martin Nicolaus. New York: International.

———. [1859] 1970. *A Contribution to the Critique of Political Economy.* Edited, introduction by Maurice Dobb. New York: International.

———. [1863*a*] 1963. *Theories of Surplus-Value, Vol. 4 of Capital,* Part 1. Translated by Emile Burns; edited by S. Ryazanskaya. Moscow: Progress.

———. [1863*b*] 1968. *Theories of Surplus-Value, Vol. 4 of Capital,* Part 2. Edited by S. Ryazanskaya. Moscow: Progress.

———. [1863*c*] 1971. *Theories of Surplus-Value, Vol. 4 of Capital,* Part 3. Translated from the German by Jack Cohen and S. W. Ryazanskaya; edited by S. W. Ryazanskaya and Richard Dixon. Moscow: Progress.

———. [1865] 1976. "Value, Price and Profit." In Marx 1976.

———. [1865] 1982. Letter to J. B. Schweitzer (24 January). In Marx and Engels 1982.

———. [1867] 1967. *Capital: A Critique of Political Economy, Vol. 1: The Process of Capitalist Production.* Edited by Frederick Engels; translated from the Third German edition by Samuel Moore and Edward Aveling. New York: International.

———. [1868*a*] 1982. Letter to Ludwig Kugelmann (11 July). In Marx and Engels 1982.

———. [1868*b*] 1982. Letter to J. B. Schweitzer (13 October). In Marx and Engels 1982.

———. [1871] 1968. *The Civil War in France.* In Marx and Engels 1968.

———. [1871] 1983. From the first draft: "The Character of the Commune." In Marx 1983.

——— . [1873] 1967. Afterword to the second German edition (24 January). In Marx [1867] 1967.

——— . [1875] 1968. "Critique of the Gotha Programme." In Marx and Engels 1968.

——— . [1877] 1982. Letter to F. A. Sorge (19 October). In Marx and Engels 1982.

——— . [1879] 1982. Letter to N. F. Danielson (10 April). In Marx and Engels 1982.

——— . [1885] 1967. *Capital: A Critique of Political Economy, Vol. 2: The Process of Circulation of Capital.* Edited by Frederick Engels. New York: International.

——— . [1894] 1967. *Capital: A Critique of Political Economy, Vol. 3: The Process of Capitalist Production as a Whole.* Edited by Frederick Engels. New York: International.

——— . 1963. *Early Writings.* Translated and edited by T. B. Bottomore; foreword by Erich Fromm. New York: McGraw-Hill.

——— . 1967. *Writings of the Young Marx on Philosophy and Society.* Edited and translated by Loyd D. Easton and Kurt H. Guddat. Garden City, N.Y.: Anchor, Doubleday.

——— . 1976. *Wage-Labour and Capital, and Value, Price and Profit.* New York: International.

——— . 1983. *The Portable Karl Marx.* Selected, translated in part, and introduction by Eugene Kamenka. New York: Viking Penguin.

Marx, Karl and Frederick Engels. [1844] 1967. *The Holy Family.* In Marx 1967.

——— . [1845-46] 1970. *The German Ideology.* Edited, introduction, by C. J. Arthur. New York: International.

——— . [1848] 1968. "Manifesto of the Communist Party." In Marx and Engels 1968.

——— . 1962. *Selected Works, Vol. 1.* Moscow: Progress.

——— . 1968. *Selected Works, in one volume.* New York: International.

——— . 1982. *Selected Correspondence, 1844-1895,* 3d rev. ed. Translated by I. Lasker; edited by S. W. Ryazanskaya. Moscow: Progress.

McCarthy, George E. 1990. *Marx and the Ancients: Classical Ethics, Social Justice, and Nineteenth-Century Political Economy.* Savage, Md.: Rowman & Littlefield.

———, ed. 1992. *Marx and Aristotle: Nineteenth-century German Social Theory and Classical Antiquity*. Savage, Md.: Rowman & Littlefield.

McCarthy, Thomas. 1978. *The Critical Theory of Jürgen Habermas*. London: Hutchinson and Company.

McLellan, David. 1970. *Marx Before Marxism*. New York: Harper & Row.

———. [1971] 1980. *The Thought of Karl Marx: An Introduction*, 2d ed. London: Macmillan.

———. 1973. *Karl Marx: His Life and Thought*. New York: Harper & Row.

———. 1979. *Marxism After Marx: An Introduction*. Boston: Houghton Mifflin.

Meek, Ronald L. 1954. "The Scottish Contribution to Marxist Sociology." In *Democracy and the Labour Movement*, edited by John Saville, pp. 84-102. London: Lawrence and Wishert Ltd.

———. [1956] 1976. *Studies in the Labor Theory of Value*, 2d ed. New York: Monthly Review.

Meikle, Scott. 1985. *Essentialism in the Thought of Karl Marx*. LaSalle, Ill.: Open Court.

Menger, Carl. [1871] 1950. *Principles of Economics*. Translated and edited by James Dingwall and Bert F. Hoselitz. Glencoe, Ill.: Free Press.

Mepham, John and David-Hillel Ruben, eds. 1979. *Issues in Marxist Philosophy, Vol. 2: Materialism*. Atlantic Highlands, N.J.: Humanities.

Merleau-Ponty, Maurice. 1973. *Adventures of the Dialectic*. Translated by Joseph Bien. Evanstan, Ill.: Northwestern University Press.

Mises, Ludwig von. [1912] 1971. *The Theory of Money and Credit*, 3d ed. New York: Foundation for Economic Education.

———. [1920] 1933. "Economic calculation in the socialist commonwealth." In Hayek [1933] 1975.

———. [1936] 1951. *Socialism: An Economic and Sociological Analysis*. Translated by J. Kahane. London: Jonathan Cape.

———. [1949] 1963. *Human Action: A Treatise on Economics*, 3d ed. rev. Chicago: Henry Regnery.

———. [1957] 1969. *Theory and History: An Interpretation of Social and Economic Evolution*. New Rochelle, N.Y.: Arlington House.

Molinari, Gustave de. [1849] 1977. *The Production of Security*. Translated by J. Huston McCulloch. New York: Center for Libertarian Studies.

Moore, Barrington. 1966. *Social Origins of Dictatorship and Democracy: Lord and Peasant in the Making of the Modern World*. Boston: Beacon.

Mouffe, Chantal, ed. 1979. *Gramsci and Marxist Theory*. London: Routledge and Kegan Paul.

Nasar, Sylvia. 1992. "Friedrich von Hayek Dies at 92; an Early Free-market Economist." *The New York Times* (24 March):D22.

Natanson, Maurice, ed. 1973. *Phenomenology and the Social Sciences*. 2 vols. Evanston, Ill.: Northwestern University Press.

Neumann, Franz. [1944] 1966. *Behemouth: The Structure and Practice of National Socialism, 1933-1944*. New York: Oxford University Press.

Nietzsche, Frederick. [1883-85] 1905. *Thus Spake Zarathustra*. Translated by Thomas Common. Introduction by Mrs. Forster-Nietzsche. New York: Modern Library, Random House.

Nisbet, Robert. 1980. "Conservatives and Libertarians: Uneasy Cousins." *Modern Age* 24, no. 1 (Winter):2-8.

Novack, George. [1969] 1971. *An Introduction to the Logic of Marxism*, 5th ed. New York: Pathfinder.

Nove, Alec. 1969. *An Economic History of the U.S.S.R.* London: Penguin.

———. 1978. *Political Economy and Soviet Socialism*. London: George Allen and Unwin.

———. 1980. *The Soviet Economic System*. London: George Allen and Unwin.

———. 1983. *The Economics of Feasible Socialism*. London: George Allen and Unwin.

O'Driscoll, Gerald P. 1977. *Economics as a Coordination Problem: The Contributions of Friedrich A. Hayek*. Kansas City: Sheed Andrews and McMeel.

Ollman, Bertell. 1976. *Alienation: Marx's Conception of Man in Capitalist Society*, 2d ed. Cambridge, England: Cambridge University Press.

———. 1979. *Social and Sexual Revolution: Essays on Marx and Reich*. Boston: South End.

———. 1993. *Dialectical Investigations*. New York: Routledge.

Ollman, Bertell and Edward Vernoff, eds. 1982. *The Left Academy: Marxist Scholarship on American Campuses*, Vol. I. New York: McGraw-Hill.

――――. 1984. *The Left Academy: Marxist Scholarship on American Campuses*, Vol. II. New York: Praeger.

――――. 1986. *The Left Academy: Marxist Scholarship on American Campuses*, Vol. III. New York: Praeger.

Piccone, Paul. 1973. "Phenomenological Marxism." *Telos* 9:3-31.

Plamenatz, John. 1975. *Karl Marx's Philosophy of Man*. Oxford: Clarendon.

Polanyi, Michael. [1958] 1962. *Personal Knowledge: Towards a Post-Critical Philosophy*. Chicago: University of Chicago.

Popper, Karl. [1940] 1963. "What Is dialectic?" In *Conjectures and Refutations*. London: Routledge and Kegan Paul.

――――. [1959] 1968. *The Logic of Scientific Discovery*. New York: Basic; London: Hutchinson.

――――. [1962*a*] 1971. *The Open Society and Its Enemies, Vol. 1: The Spell of Plato*. Princeton: Princeton University Press.

――――. [1962*b*] 1971. *The Open Society and Its Enemies, Vol. 2: The High Tide of Prophecy: Hegel, Marx, and the Aftermath*. Princeton: Princeton University Press.

――――. [1969] 1976. "The Logic of the Social Sciences." In *The Positivist Dispute in German Sociology*, translated by Glyn Adey and David Frisby. London: Heinemann Educational.

――――. [1975] 1981. "The Rationality of Scientific Revolutions." In Hacking 1981: pp. 80-106.

Poulantzas, Nicos. 1973. *Political Power and Social Classes*. Translation editor Timothy O'Hagan. Atlantic Highlands, N.J.: Humanities.

――――. 1978. *State, Power, Socialism*. Translated by Patrick Camiller. London: NLB and Verso.

Prychitko, David L. 1991. *Marxism and Workers' Self-Management: The Essential Tension*. New York: Greenwood.

Radosh, Ronald and Murray N. Rothbard. 1972. *A New History of Leviathan*. New York: E. P. Dutton.

Rand, Ayn. 1957. *Atlas Shrugged*. New York: Random House; New American Library.

――――. 1961. *For the New Intellectual*. New York: New American Library.

――――. 1964. *The Virtue of Selfishness: A New Concept of Egoism*. New York: New American Library.

————. 1990. *Introduction to Objectivist Epistemology*, 2d expanded ed. New York: New American Library.

Ricoeur, Paul. [1971] 1977. "The Model of the Text: Meaningful Action Considered as a Text." In Dallmayr and McCarthy 1977: pp. 316-24.

Roelofs, H. Mark. 1976. *Ideology and Myth in American Politics*. Boston: Little, Brown.

Rothbard, Murray N. [1956] 1977. "Toward a Reconstruction of Utility and Welfare Economics." *C.L.S. Occasional Paper Series, 3*. New York: The Center for Libertarian Studies.

————. [1963] 1975. *America's Great Depression*, 3d ed. Kansas City: Sheed and Ward.

————. 1970. *Man, Economy and State*. One complete volume. Los Angeles: Nash.

————. [1970] 1977. *Power and Market: Government and the Economy*. Kansas City: Sheed Andrews and McMeel.

————. [1976] 1980. "The New Deal and the International Monetary System." In *The Great Depression and New Deal Monetary Policy*. San Francisco: Cato Institute.

————. 1978*a*. "Economic Depressions: Their Cause and Cure." In *The Austrian Theory of the Trade Cycle*, edited by Richard M. Ebeling. New York: Center for Libertarian Studies.

————. 1978*b*. *For a New Liberty: The Libertarian Manifesto*, rev. ed. New York: Collier.

————. 1987. "The Consequences of Human Action: Intended or Unintended?" *The Free Market* (May): 3.

Ryan, Alan, ed. 1973. *The Philosophy of Social Explanation*. Oxford Readings in Philosophy. Oxford: Oxford University Press.

Sayer, Derek. 1983. *Marx's Method: Ideology, Science and Critique in Capital*, 2d ed. Atlantic Highlands, N.J.: Humanities.

Sciabarra, Chris M. 1987. "The Crisis of Libertarian Dualism." *Critical Review* 1, no. 4 (Fall):86-99.

————. 1988*a*. *Toward a Radical Critique of Utopianism: Dialectics and Dualism in the Works of Friedrich Hayek, Murray Rothbard and Karl Marx*. Doctoral dissertation, New York University. Ann Arbor, Michigan: University Microfilms International.

————. 1988*b*. "A Reply to Tibor Machan." *Critical Review* 2, nos. 2 & 3 (Spring/Summer):227-29.

———. 1988c. "Marx on the Precipice of Utopia." Review of Kevin Brien's *Marx, Reason and the Art of Freedom*. *Critical Review* 2, no. 4 (Fall):76-81.

———. 1989. "Ayn Rand's Critique of Ideology." *Reason Papers* no. 14 (Spring):32-44.

———. 1990. "From Aristotle to Marx." Review of Scott Meikle's *Essentialism in the Thought of Karl Marx*. *Critical Review* 4, nos. 1-2 (Winter/Spring):61-73.

———. 1995. *Ayn Rand: The Russian Radical*. University Park, Pa.: Penn State Press.

Selsam, Howard and Harry Martel, eds. 1963. *Reader in Marxist Philosophy from the Writings of Marx, Engels, and Lenin*. New York: International.

Shaffer, Butler D. [1975] 1976. "Violence as a Product of Imposed Order." *Studies in Law 4*. Menlo Park, Calif.: Institute for Humane Studies.

Sharp, Gene. 1973. *The Politics of Nonviolent Action, part 1: Power and Struggle*. Boston: Porter Sargent.

———. 1980. *Social Power and Political Freedom*. Boston: Porter Sargent.

Sowell, Thomas. 1985. *Marxism: Philosophy and Economics*. New York: William Morrow.

Steele, David Ramsay. 1992. *From Marx to Mises: Post-Capitalist Society and the Challenge of Economic Calculation*. LaSalle, Ill.: Open Court.

Sweezy, Paul, ed. [1949] 1975. *Karl Marx and the Close of His System*. Clifton, N.J.: Augustus M. Kelley.

Tar, Zoltan. 1977. *The Frankfurt School: The Critical Theories of Max Horkheimer and Theodor W. Adorno*. New York: John Wiley and Sons.

Therborn, Goran. 1976. *Science, Class and Society: On the Formation of Sociology and Historical Materialism*. London: NLB.

———. 1984. "The Frankfurt School." In Marcus and Tar, 1984: pp. 343-74.

Thomas, Paul. 1980. *Karl Marx and the Anarchists*. London: Routledge and Kegan Paul.

Thompson, John B. and David Held, eds. 1982. *Habermas: Critical Debates*. Cambridge, Mass.: MIT Press.

Tomlinson, Jim. 1990. *Hayek and the Market*. Winchester, Mass.: Pluto.

Trotsky, Leon. [1924] 1960. *Literature and Revolution.* New York: Russell and Russell.

Vaughn, Karen. 1980*a.* "John Locke's Theory of Property." *Literature of Liberty* 3, no. 1 (Spring):5-37.

———. 1980*b. John Locke: Economist and Social Scientist.* Chicago: University of Chicago Press.

———. 1982. "On the Tradition of Spontaneous Order." *Literature of Liberty* 5, no. 4 (Winter):9-11.

Vorhies, Frank. 1989. "Marx on Money and Crises." *Critical Review* 3, nos. 3 & 4 (Summer/Fall):531-41.

Wainwright, Hilary. 1994. *Arguments for a New Left: Answering the Free Market Right.* Oxford: Blackwell.

Wartofsky, Marx W. 1983. "From Genetic Epistemology to Historical Epistemology: Kant, Marx, and Piaget." In *Piaget and the Foundations of Knowledge,* edited by Lynn S. Liben. Hillsdale, N.J.: Lawrence Erlbaum Associates, pp. 1-17.

Weber, Max. [1949] 1977. "'Objectivity' in Social Science and Social Policy." In Dallmayr and McCarthy 1977: pp. 24-37.

Weiss, John, ed. 1969. *Nazis and Fascists in Europe, 1918-1945.* Chicago: Quadrangle.

Wootton, Barbara. 1945. *Freedom Under Planning.* Chapel Hill: University of North Carolina Press.

Index

A

abstraction, 55-56, 132 n.5
Adorno, Theodor, 101-2, 144 n.10
Alexander, Jeffrey, 70-71
alienation, 65, 89, 91, 109
Althusser, Louis, 6, 91, 124 n.11,
   138 n.46
anarchism
   and anarchocapitalism, 23, 133
      n.15
   and libertarian socialism, 58
   Marx's critique of, 58
Aquinas, Thomas, 139 n.59,
   139 n.60
Aristotle, 92, 100
   as dialectical thinker, 3-4, 79-
      82, 123 n.4, 123 n.5, 139
      n.60, 139 n.67, 141-42
      n.38
atomism, 5, 14, 16-18, 111
   Aristotle's opposition to, 81
   and capitalism, 55
   defined, 21
   and dualism, 23
   vs. organicism, 20, 22, 127 n.41
   Scottish liberals' opposition to,
      63
Austrian school of economics, 11,
   38, 75-78, 91-95, 126 n.35,
   128 n.50, 137 n.34, 141 n.37,
   141-42 n.38, 142 n.40, 146
   n.49
Avineri, Shlomo, 71, 91, 125 n.12

B

Bakunin, Mikhail A., 58
Barry, Norman, 38, 50
Bartley, W. W., 34
"base" and "superstructure," 7,
   70, 72-74, 78-79, 138 n.46
Bastiat, Frederic, 15
Bernstein, Richard J., 80
Blanshard, Brand
   as Absolute Idealist, 27-28, 47
   Brien on, 128 n.53
   on internal relations, 20, 25, 28
   on internal vs. external rela-
      tions, 24
Boehm-Bawerk, Eugen von, 92,
   139 n.60, 142 n.40
Boettke, Peter J., 143 n.53, 147
   n.8
Branden, Nathaniel, 131 n.6
Brien, Kevin, 7, 128 n.53
Browning, Robert, 1
Burke, Edmund, 12-15, 19, 61, 63,
   125 n.10
   See also conservatism
Business cycles, 65-66, 76-78, 137
   n.34

C

Cabet, Étienne, 57
calculation debate, 92-93, 113,
   141 n.35